Being Ninety

Old West Monsters and A Texas Poet's Life

Donald Mace Williams

STONEY CREEK PUBLISHING
Stoneycreekpublishing.com

Stoney Creek Publishing
A Member of the Texas Book Consortium

Published by
Stoney Creek Publishing
stoneycreekpublishing.com

Copyright © 2022 Donald Mace Williams
Distributed by Texas A&M University Press
ISBN (paperback): 979-8-9864078-2-1
ISBN (ebook): 979-8-9864078-4-5
Library of Congress: 2022914337

Interior design by
Vivian Freeman Chaffin
vivian.freeman@yellowrosetype.com

Cover design by
Martha Williams Nichols
aMuse Productions, Fort Collins, Colorado

Back Cover Photo by
John Newland

Printed in the United States

❦

Wolfe was first published in *Rattle* magazine (Winter, 2008). In 2009, *Rattle* brought it out as a separate chapbook. In 2017, it was published in *Wolfe and Other Poems* by Wundor Editions, Ltd. (London). A passage from *Being Ninety* was published online by *National Review* (April 4, 2021). The author is grateful to all those sources for permission to reprint the two works.

TABLE OF CONTENTS

Wolfe

Old West Monsters

AUTHOR'S NOTE

This is a cowboy story, and I wrote it to stand alone as such. But I think it does become apparent before long, also, that the poem has echoes of something else: *Beowulf,* or the best-known parts of it. In that poem, Hrothgar, ruler of the Danes, builds a mighty beer hall. The sounds of revelry from it infuriate the monster Grendel, who raids the hall, carrying off thirty thanes. He continues the raids for years. Then Beowulf, a young Swedish warrior who has heard of the raids, arrives to help Hrothgar. He waits for Grendel at night, wrestles with him, and tears off the monster's arm. Grendel flees, mortally wounded. Hrothgar rewards Beowulf richly.

But then Grendel's mother comes to avenge her son and kills Aeschere, the close friend of Hrothgar. Beowulf seeks her out in her underwater den, struggles with her, and, though his trusted sword fails him, eventually kills her. Honored as the deliverer of the Danes, he goes home to a life of fame and honor.

I have thought of Tom Rogers as the ranchland equivalent of Hrothgar (the name Roger is derived from Hrothgar). Other more-or-less matched characters are Aeschere and Ashley, Wealtheow and Elsa, Unferth and Humphrey, and of course Beowulf and Billy Wolfe.

Toward the end of *Being Ninety,* the companion piece to this poem, I have gone into somewhat more detail about *Wolfe* and how I came to write it.

WOLFE

Fat Herefords grazed on rich brown grass.
Tom Rogers watched three winters pass,
Then, all his ranch paid off, designed
A bunkhouse, biggest of its kind
In that wide stretch of Caprock lands,
To house the army of top hands
That rising markets and good rain
Forced and allowed him to maintain.
At night sometimes a cowboy sang
Briefly to a guitar's soft twang
While others talked, wrote letters home,
Or stared into brown-bottle foam.
Rogers, white-haired as washed gyp rock,
Stood winding Cyclops, the tall clock,
One night and heard the sleepy sound
Of song across the strip of ground
Between the bunkhouse and the house.
He smiled and dropped his hand. Near Taos,
At night, pensive and wandering out
From camp, a young surveyor-scout,
He had heard singing just that thin
Rise from the pueblo. Go on in,
A voice kept saying, but he stood,
One arm hooked round a cottonwood
For strength until, ashamed, he whirled

And strode back to the measured world.
Strange, how that wild sound in the night
Had drawn him, who was hired to sight
Down lines that tamed. So now, he thought,
Winding until the spring came taut,
This clock, this house, these wide fenced plains,
These little towns prove up our pains.
He went to bed, blew out the light
On the nightstand, said a good night
To Elsa, and dropped off to sleep
Hearing a last faint twang.
                                    From deep
In the fierce breaks came a reply,
A drawn-out keening, pitched as high
And savage as if cowboy songs,
To strange, sharp ears, summed up all wrongs
Done to the wilderness by men,
Fences, and cows. With bared teeth then,
Ears back, the apparition skulked
Across the ridges toward the bulked,
Repulsive forms of house and shed,
Till now not neared. The next dawn's red
Revealed a redder scene. The pen
Where calving heifers were brought in
In case of need lay strewn and gory,
Each throat and belly slashed, a story
Of rage, not hunger; nothing gone
But one calf's liver. His face drawn,
Rogers bent close to find a track
In the hard dirt. Then he drew back,
Aghast. Though it was mild and fair,
He would always thereafter swear
There hung above that broad paw print

With two deep claw holes a mere hint,
The sheerest wisp, of steam. He stood
Silent. When finally he could,
He said, "Well, I guess we all know
What done this. No plain lobo, though.
I've seen a few. They never killed
More than to get their belly filled.
This one's a devil. Look at that."
He toed a carcass. Where the fat
And lean had been flensed, red and white,
From a front leg, a second bite
Had crushed the bone above the knee.
By ones and twos men leaned to see
With open mouths. A clean, dark hole
At one side punched clear through the bole.
"That's no tooth, it's a railroad spike,"
One cowboy breathed. Or else it's like,
Tom Rogers thought, a steel-tipped arrow
Such as once pierced him, bone and marrow,
Mid-calf when, riding in advance
Of wagons on the trail to Grants,
Attacked, he turned and in the mud
Escaped with one boot full of blood.
At least the Indians had a cause,
He thought. This thing came from the draws
To kill and waste, no more. He spat
And said, "I'll get hitched up." At that,
Two cowboys jumped to do the chore
While from the pile by the back door
Others, jaws set, began to carry
Cottonwood logs onto the prairie
Where horses dragged the grim night's dead
Like travois to their fiery bed.

Rogers, with hands in pockets, stood
And said, "That barbecue smells good."
But the half-smile he struggled for
Turned on him like a scimitar
And cowboys, sensing, kept their eyes
Down and said nothing. By sunrise
Of the next day the word was out
By mouth and telegraph about
The beast that crept out of the dark
And slaughtered like a land-bound shark,
Evil, bloodthirsty, monstrous. Soon
The story was that the full moon
Caused that four-legged beast to rise
On two feet and with bloodshot eyes
To roam the plains in search of prey
Like some cursed half-man. In one day
Three of Rogers' good cowboys quit,
No cowards but not blessed with wit
To fathom the unknown, and more
Kept glancing at the bunkhouse door
At night as if, next time, the thing
Might burst inside. "Hey, man, don't sing,"
One said as a guitar came out.
There did seem, thinking back, no doubt
That music must have been what stirred
The anger out there. Some had heard
The answer. They agreed the sound
Came after Ashley's fingers found
The highest note of that night's strumming.
"Play it again you know what's coming,"
Said one named Humphrey. Ashley, who
Like Humphrey had seen Rogers through
The hard first years of ranching there,

Loyal and lean, kept guessing where
The thing would strike next. Every night
He rode out to some downwind site
Deep in the wildest breaks and waited.
Nothing. But then, as if so fated,
Homeward at dawn, on this high rim
Or in that gulch he found the grim
Fang-torn remains of cow or calf.
Before long Rogers' herd was half
What it had been. If half his hands
Had not already found the bands
Of loyalty no longer served
And drawn their pay and left, unnerved
By these unholy deeds, their boss
Would have no choice, with nightly loss
Of his best stock, but cut his force
Like cutting calves out with a horse.
Ashley, of course, would always stay
Though everything else went its way.
Those two had cowboyed in all weather
And for a while had fought together
Against the Indians' dwindling ranks,
Ending between the steep red banks
Of Palo Duro, that brief fight
That put the tribes to final flight,
Horseless and foodless. The next day,
Colonel Mackenzie took the way
Surest to keep the foe from turning
Back to his killing, theft, and burning.
He gathered his captains about,
Said, "Take these Indian horses out
And shoot them." Rogers was the head
Of Ashley's squad. The soldiers led

Horse after snorting horse away,
A thousand head to kill. They say
The white bones made, in later years,
A heap like bent and bleaching spears.
They might as well have been spears. Shorn
Of their chief means of war, forlorn,
Hungry, and whipped, the sad tribes found
The long paths to that plotted ground
Decreed as home for them, no more
To hunt and plunder. From that store
Of battle memories, of thirst
And weariness they shared, of worst
And best, noncom and soldier grew
To boss and hand when they were through
Clearing the way for settlement,
Theirs and the thousands like them, bent
On owning, taming that wild land.
Now, one had grown a wise top hand
In middle years, tough, and yet given
To strumming music, sometimes driven
To ride out when the moon sat round
And dark on the far rim and sound
A sadness he could not explain,
As if pity and guilt had lain
Unknown through the long interval
Since the last moon had hung that full
Of melancholy, even fear.

But Rogers, finding year by year
That sitting on a horse straight-spined
Was harder, most days stayed behind
While cowboys went out riding fence
Or pulling calves. His recompense

For his lost saddle was a chair
On his long, screened-in back porch, where
He rocked and watched his herd on grass
That not long back felt no hooves pass
But buffaloes', there where the brim
Of Palo Duro Canyon, dim
And distant, showed. He was content.
Then came the night marauding. Bent
Or not, he started work again,
Helping fill in for the lost men
Who left for where no ghostly thing
Came from the jumbled breaks to bring
Slaughter and ruin. So it went,
The kills still coming, no trap meant
For wolf or bear seeming to draw
Even a glance. One cowboy saw
A skulking form outlined at dusk
Once, and he claimed the creature's tusk
Far off flashed like a polished blade.
He left. A dozen, shaken, stayed.

Then one May morning, breakfast done,
Rogers sat rocking in the sun,
His back so bad for the first time
He knew he couldn't make the climb
Into the saddle. Elsa said,
"Listen. Was that a horse?" Her head
Was tilted toward the lonely road,
And soon a knock came. Her face glowed.
Who could that be? It was a thrill
To have a visitor. "Sit still,"
She said, and put aside her sewing
To get the door. He watched her going,

Lightfoot, and smiled. Soon, down the hall,
Slow footsteps came. The man was tall
And younger than his voice had seemed,
A stripling almost, narrow-beamed
And -shouldered, while a high-bridged nose
Ground sharp enough to slice bread rose
Startling in features cut so thin
His smile seemed too broad for his chin.
A boy. Still, Rogers thought, his gaze
Is sure and hard. He's known the ways
Of mean men and wild storms. "Sit down,"
He said. "I can't get up." His brown,
Hard hand reached out, and when they shook,
The young man's grip confirmed his look.
He sat with scuffed boots and bared head.
"My name is Billy Wolfe," he said.
"I hear you've got a problem here."
Rogers smiled. "Well, your name comes near
To what it is. Can you ride? Rope?"
"Yes, sir, a little. But I'd hope
Mainly to help you folks get rid
Of your calf-killer." Rogers slid
Wincing around to look head-on.
"The word about this must have gone
A long way, since I've never heard
Your name or seen your face." "The word
Has got to Kansas, I know that
Because it's where I hang my hat."
He smiled again. "The paper claimed
It walked upright and its breath flamed."

He stopped, for Elsa, slim and graceful, had stepped through
The door between the porch and kitchen with a blue-

Enameled coffee pot and china cup and saucer,
She straight-formed, blue-eyed, with a pink shawl thrown
    across her
Shoulders; and shaking neat white hair she said, "No, please
Don't get up. Do you take cream? Sugar?" On his knees
He balanced cup and saucer as she poured. She filled
Her husband's cup and went out, leaving all talk stilled

While both men angled their thoughts back
From Elsa to the thing whose track,
Rogers informed him, was so broad
It had to be a male's, long-clawed,
Deep-sunken. "If you want to know,
It's not your plain old mean lobo,"
Rogers went on. "It's something strange.
My top hand thinks it hates the range
Itself, now that it's fenced and stocked,
And men and houses." Rogers rocked
And sipped his coffee. "It's so strong,
It crushed a leg and left this long
A channel in the bone. No tooth
On any wolf does that." The youth
Leaned forward, elbows on his knees.
"Sounds like a throwback, one of these
They dig up bones of now and then.
Or else..." He shrugged, sat back again,
And soon the two had made a deal,
So much a month. "But if you heal
Us of this plague," said Rogers, "son,
Just name your price." They shook hands: done.
When Wolfe had put his horse away
And stowed his things out back, the day
Was getting on toward noon. The men

Began to drift in, wash up, then
Sit waiting till the meal was ready,
The new man, too. They liked his steady
But modest gaze, though no one spoke
More than a few words. The mood broke,
Though, when the next man came and sat.
"So you're a wolf's bane." Humphrey spat.
"Ever hear of the XIT?
They had some guys there, used to be,
That took a light and crawled up in
There where the mama had her den
And when her eyes shone back they aimed
Between and shot her. So they claimed.
I'm sure you've done that." Billy said,
"A time or two," his smile still spread
Across his narrow face and past,
His voice light, though his eyes held fast
Till Humphrey shrugged and turned his back.
Lunch done, the new man got his tack
And went out working with the others,
Helping to roust some calves and mothers
Out of the brush. "I'll tell you, now,"
He said, "can we put every cow
And calf up in that one big pen
Tonight—well, not the whole bunch, then;
The newest ones will do—I think
He might just pay a call." A wink.
Ashley, who rode beside him, thought,
All right, I guess it's this that brought
This kid so far from home. Let's try
Whatever notion happens by
And see our Billy Wolfe in action.
They rounded up some minor fraction

Of those few new calves still around.
They and their mothers soon were bound
For that one pen where something first
Had crept, fangs and eyes bright, and burst
Out of the dark with teeth like spears
To strike and kill. Then Wolfe said, "Here's
My bed tonight." "Here?" Ashley said,
Amazed. "Yes, and to make the bed
I need some fat and one fresh hide."
"None here," said Ashley. "You could ride
Along the road and ask the neighbor."
He saw just what the new man's labor
Was going to be, though the mere thought
Gave him the creeps. Wolfe rode and brought
The things he needed, given free
For what the neighbor hoped to see:
One sheepish tenderfoot at dawn
Washing off what had been smeared on,
No beast or slaughter to be found.

At dark, Wolfe curled up on the ground
Naked under the hide, hair, face,
And body fat-smeared to erase
The man-smell, knife and Colt close by,
A cowlike heap, he hoped, to lie
In ambush. Soon, at his request,
The sound of music drifted west,
Voice and guitar, high notes and all,
Ashley's best songs. Wolfe heard the call,
High-pitched and savage, that replied,
And felt a shiver deep inside,
A thrill of wonder, not quite fear,
Of mystery soon to be clear.

And then, thus tensed to meet the threat
And covered with discomfort, yet
This was a man still of an age
When rest ruled other needs. The sage
Around him glimmered in the moon
And from the bunkhouse Ashley's tune
Lulled strangely. Wolfe succumbed, and slept.
The moon climbed, shrinking.
                                Now there crept
In from the wilds, his eyes aglow,
Tongue out at one side, belly low,
A monster of primeval dreams,
Of Folsom women's moonrise screams.
Once through the fence and in the pen
He sprang without a pause. Till then
The cattle had stood still, asleep,
But now they heard him gather, leap,
And bring a month-old calf to earth.
The blood smell squeezed them like a girth
Against the far fence, snorting. Now
The predator raced toward the cow
He thought he saw sprawled in the dirt
Off to the side, sick, dead, or hurt.
Just then the hooves and snorting woke
The man who lay there. Billy broke
Out of his cover as the teeth
Slashed through the hide, and from beneath
Himself he pulled his hunting knife,
Knowing his gun could take a life
Other than what he in the dark
Had meant. Through arc on flashing arc
The long blade struck, as in surprise
The beast fought free, from his pale eyes

Moonlight reflecting fear and pain.
Limping, he fled onto the plain.
His pistol out now, Billy followed,
Firing, until the night had swallowed
The sounds of flight. Shortly the hush
Gave way to waking yells. A rush
Of booted feet came next, and then
Where Wolfe stood gun in hand, the men
Out of the bunkhouse stood around him
In the dark, peering. "So you found him,"
One youngster said. Wolfe, with a laugh,
Said, "Well, he found me. And one calf.
I got him some, though, with the knife."
Here came—slowly, to guard the life
Of a cupped candle flame—the man
Who had scoffed, Humphrey. Where he ran,
The beast had left, the flame showed, red,
Deep pools of blood, and by the bed
Where Wolfe had slept, a patch, dark-haired,
Which, he surmised, the knife had pared
In one slash from a shoulder, lay
Hair up, still bleeding, on the clay.
Silent, mouths open, cowboys stood
And stared. One said, "The thing done good
To walk away with that chunk gone."
But Ashley knelt as somehow drawn
To what lay there, and dropped his head
To see. "Just like a scalp," he said
Half to himself, time and again.
Soon from the house to join his men
Rogers came hobbling. When he learned
What Wolfe had done for him, he turned
And by the dim light just descried

Bare, shivering skin. "Son, get inside
And have a hot bath—melt that grease
And warm your bones. You've brought us peace,
You know. Pneumonia's no fair pay."
By first gold light of the next day
Three men traced where the beast had bled
In flight and found the dried pools led
To just the sheerest, wildest drop
In the whole canyon. From the top,
Bending, Wolfe saw a claw-scuffed streak
Down the face halfway to the creek,
Vanishing where a ledge thrust out
Beneath an overhang. No doubt
The thing had crawled into its lair,
Wolfe said. "Likely it's died in there."
Caught out somehow without a rope,
No one would climb down that steep slope
To make sure, but the brightest joy
Filled Ashley, Humphrey, and "this boy,"
As Humphrey called him, now with pride,
On the ride home. They found, inside,

Breakfast awaiting them. Elsa, her slender legs
Gracefully rushing, brought hotcakes and syrup, eggs,
And homemade sausage for all hands. Tom Rogers spoke,
A rare occurrence at a meal. "The curse is broke,"
He said to all, "thanks be to God and this kid's arm—
This man's, I mean. Now I won't have to make a farm,
God help us, of this spread. Billy, I hope you'll stay
And help work calves. But when you do go on your way
I want you riding on that little sorrel mare
Of mine. The saddle, too, that's studs were made down there

In Mexico." He waved a hand
To stop Wolfe's protest. Cowboys scanned
Their plates as if for something lost,
Not speaking. Still, somehow there crossed
The stretched-out table a faint glow,
An aura, serving well to show
Approval and acceptance. Then,
The special meal done, all the men,
The newest one among them, rode
Out where the late-spring sunlight showed
In crisp detail a threat-free range.
That night, nobody thought it strange
When in deep thought, with his guitar,
Ashley rode westward, out as far
As they could hear across the plains,
Singing his melancholy strains.
Nor were the sleeping men aware
Till morning that his bunk lay there
Unused. They checked. His horse was gone.
Wordlessly in the crimson dawn
Humphrey rode out. He came back pale,
Hitching his horse to the long rail
By the back porch where in his chair
Rogers was gazing at the fair,
Newly unburdened land he claimed,
Land he and now young Wolfe had tamed
And made safe grazing for his herd.
Then Humphrey stepped in with the word
That changed all back to a dark time.
Some of the men helped Rogers climb
Into the saddle. At the rim
They stopped and looked far down. "That's him,"
Said Humphrey, "downslope from the horse."

Dismounting, he worked out a course
And with five others picked his way
Steeply to where the body lay.
In peril, aided by a rope,
They brought it up the wall-like slope,
The crushed guitar, too. Ashley's throat
Was ripped wide, and his denim coat
Hung soaked in blood. "That was no fall,"
Said Rogers. "That thing did it all.
It got his throat and pulled him off
Over the rim and in the trough."
Humphrey said, yes, the horse had been
Ripped the same way, and, falling then,
Had left a red trail down the wall.
He pointed. One more thing. The tall
Fretboard of the guitar showed, clean
And deep, toothmarks like that one seen
In a calf's bone a few weeks back.
"Down there I saw a bloody track,"
Said Humphrey. "It was wide, this wide,
But wouldn't look big put beside
That other one we saw. I'd say
This was the female. Stuck away
In that cliff where the first one crawled
She'll have a half-grown litter."
                                    Called
Now from the back where he had hung
Unwilling to intrude, the young
New hand moved forward, took his place
In front, saw how the canyon face
Was blood-streaked far down, and, himself
Clambering down, each inch-deep shelf
And narrow crack a handhold, studied

The track, the horse, the rocks still bloodied
That many hundred feet below.
On top again, he watched as, slow
And hushed, men lashed their foreman-friend
To two spliced planks and laid each end
Across a horse, then side by side,
Still wordless, set out on the ride
Back to the house. Wolfe stayed behind
And said to Rogers, "I'll go find
That den and get her." Rogers said,
"You know I'd love to have her dead.
It would be more for Ashley's sake
Than for the ranch. Make no mistake,
It wasn't any accident
He came out here last night. He meant
To make his peace somehow. I knew
That man a long time. We've been through
Battles that afterward he'd sit
Just like we'd lost. He never fit—
It's hard to say—never approved
Of how we all came, fought, and moved
Onto the land. And still he fought
As hard as any. He was taught
That way. We all were." Rogers turned
And looked down-canyon where sunburned
Red walls gave way to jumbled gloom.
"Son, look there. That's the crack of doom.
I mean it. No one goes down there.
I tried. Something about the air
Made my horse snort and balk. Don't go.
She may be satisfied. If so,
We'll carry on and stay away
From cliffs at night. If not, the day

May come when I give up, sell out
For nothing, and go turnabout
Back to the city. Let her be.
I wouldn't like to stand and see
Your body hauled up from the floor
Like that one." Rogers said no more,
And on the ride back neither spoke.
But when the first red sunlight broke
Over the plains the morning past
The funeral, Wolfe and the last
Remaining hands—for three had gone,
Afraid, since slaughter had moved on
From calves to men—took matches, rope,
And one thick candle to the slope,
Rather, the cliff, in which, they knew,
Hid by a rock bulge from their view,
The den lay. Wolfe wore gloves, thick, tough,
And long. A pocket held enough
Forty-five rounds for one reload
Of his old pistol, and there glowed,
Stuck in his belt, a polished blade,
The one that some days past had made
A budding legend of the man
Who bore it. When the day began
Wolfe left his other things behind,
Few that they were, with a note signed
"Your loving son," in Rogers' care.

Rogers had chosen not to share
The vigil at the canyon wall.
"Good luck," he said, and that was all—
Nothing like, "I'll say you a prayer,"
Though that was what he, in his chair,

Did say that morning as the sun
Climbed and no word came. More than one
Of those who waited on the rim
Did likewise, silent, when from him
Who'd calmly slipped over the side
With one end of a long rope tied
Around an ankle so, in case,
He could be dragged from that dark place,
There came no tug, no sign, no shout,
No shot. "We'll have to pull him out,"
One cowboy said. Minutes before,
Though it seemed hours, they had no more
Been able to observe him sliding
And squirming down, the rock face hiding
His form just where the den must be,
Below the overhang. A tree,
A cedar, seeming set in rock
With some great hammer, helped to block
The view from overhead. They stood
And waited. Wolfe, as best he could,
Bent over, standing on the ledge
Beneath the shelf and at the edge
Of what was still a steep descent,
And at the base saw what had meant
To slaughter him. Huge, fierce, he lay
Where he had dropped, dead, on the way
Back to his den. With awe and pride
Wolfe saw the wound in his great side.
That, Wolfe thought, is what I was meant
To do. And there was more. He bent
To see a dark hole in the cliff.
"So there you are," he said. A sniff
Told him the den was occupied.

He struck a match and with the side
Of that great gulch to block the breeze
Lighted the wick, now on his knees,
Then lay out flat and, gun ahead
In one hand, candle flickering red
Inside the dark, stale tunnel, squirmed
Far in until his eyes confirmed
What he already knew was there.
Hate-reddened, piercing, a fixed glare
Answered his flame. Farther apart
Than any eyes known to his art,
Yet they stared at the alien light
Straight on, as if their focused might
Could burn it backward on their own.
Though unlike any Wolfe had known,
They were still eyes, still in a cave,
And thus familiar. Neither brave
Nor frightened, candle held out front
As on a many a routine hunt,
His pistol cocked, Wolfe aimed between
The eyes and squeezed.
                                    The gun had seen
Long years of use and never failed
Till now. In that dark shaft Wolfe paled
To hear the click. Four, five times more
He tried, then to the rocky floor
Let the gun drop. Twisting, his life
In peril now, he jerked the knife
Out of his belt. Too late. The stroke
Of hammer against steel pin broke
On wild ears in that deep home place
Like desecration and disgrace,
And with the violated rage

Of the last tenant of an age
When cornered and invaded there
The beast sprang. Wolfe could feel the air
Hot with its breath. Charging, it uttered
A low growl. As the candle guttered
Wolfe let it drop. In darkness then
He felt the great strength once again
Of such a brute as neither he
Nor any man had thought to be
Alive, a hostile, stubborn force,
Hating man and man's westward course.
The fierce jaws closed on Wolfe's left wrist
And shook it. With a frantic twist
Wolfe freed himself before the ranks
Of spikes quite pierced his forearm, thanks
To those thick gauntlets, and he brought
The knife up, slashing where he thought
The neck would be, using his strength
The best he could while stretched full length
In the tight shaft. The beast retreated
Scarcely a foot and then repeated
Her charge. Heavy as any man
You would see on the street, she ran
Against his slashes with her own,
A massive thrust of tooth, fur, bone.
And this time, even as he fought
For life, Wolfe knew the damage wrought
By his long blade, for on his hand
He felt his foe's blood like a brand,
Hotter than human blood or skin.
But weakened though she should have been,
The beast bore down on him with power
So great she arched his back. A shower

Of knife-blade sparks, struck from a rock,
Lit up the shaft. In the full lock
Of struggle, he yet, in that flash,
Saw the deep wound, and one more slash,
It seemed to him, struck home. A shove
And a last knife blow, from above,
Must surely snuff, at last, the glow
Of those red eyes. No. Wounded so,
Powered by hate, she managed yet
To spring just as Wolfe, weary, let
His knife hand drop. He took the weight
Head-on, defenseless, heard the great
Last sigh she gave, and felt her blood
In a full, seething, pulsing flood
Hot on his head and shoulders. Then
She lay still. From the waiting men
Above him, in the silenced cave
Wolfe heard calls. With his foot he gave
The rope a tug. There came a cheer
In answer. He pushed up to peer
Over the body by the light
Of the rekindled flame. The sight
He had expected was not there:
No eyes from deeper in the lair
Glowed back at him. So that was all.
No young ones, Wolfe saw. Since the wall
Squeezed him so close, he squirmed out then,
Untied the rope, waved at the men
On top, and crawled back in. He tied
The body up, and on its side,
Straining, dragged it into the light,
Then stood and marveled at the sight
Of such a creature, bulky, broad,

With fangs, exposed in death, that awed
Even him, and for just a breath

He felt a touch of pity at that great thing's death,
Almost regretted having had to be the one
To bring it on, as if somehow what he had done
Had caused the end of more than just one life. He turned

Away then, shrugging. He had earned
Rogers his ranch back; he had won
Revenge for Ashley's death; had done
His job well, and was being paid
Already in the loud cheers laid
All down the cliff from men who watched
As he came into view. Blood-splotched
He clambered. Men who felt unmanned
By show pushed now to shake his hand,
Not caring that theirs came back red.
"It's mostly hers, not mine," Wolfe said.
Three took the rope in hand and hauled
To no effect. A fourth. Enthralled
At last they laid the body out
And stood in awe. Then came a shout:
"Here comes the boss." When he was there
They helped him down. In the clear air
Of triumph and new hope he stood
By what had killed and no more would,
And men, amazed, saw that his eyes
Were full of tears. "Everything dies,"
He said, half to himself, then turned,
Shaking it off. "Say, kid, you've earned

Your keep today," he said, and shook Wolfe's hand. They stacked
A pile of cedar brush, his men, and on it racked,
Six of them, grunting, the huge body. Then they rode
Back to the house, an hour away, and in the mode
Of Christmas or Thanksgiving all hands celebrated
That noon with Elsa's festive best. When all were sated,
Rogers rapped on his iced-tea glass and made Wolfe stand.
"I want to say," he said, "this man has saved the land
From going back to waste or else under the plow.
From what he tells me he'll be moving onward now,
Looking for other wild beasts' dens to crawl into.
Well, just to make it easier the next time through,
Here's a new Colt that's almost guaranteed to shoot.
And here's a check that might not bounce." Billy stood mute,
Embarrassed, squeezing out at last a "Thank you, boss."
There was no more to-do till sunset fell across
The flat west and all hands had had the evening meal.
With neighbors then they all rode westward. Spur on heel
For the occasion, all sat silent, looking on
While Rogers was helped down and stiffly, having drawn
A box of matches from his pocket, waited till
The mood of darkness, distance, and the evening chill
Seemed right, the body at the brink outlined in black
Against the canyon mysteries; and he thought back
To that alluring music from the pueblo. Glad
Not to have yielded, proud of everything he had,
And yet somehow unsure, he shook himself, then bent
And struck a match. Soon, bright and red as wild eyes, went
Out from the rim a signal that upon that pyre
Lay all that had fought settlers, cattle, and barbed wire.
And in the crowd, Wolfe, though impassive, knew the flame
Was justly wafting everywhere his early fame.

Being Ninety

A Texas Poet's Life

FOREWORD

By Joe Holley

The poet and essayist May Sarton observed that old age is "a foreign country with an unknown language to the young and even to the middle-aged." Donald Mace Williams, now in his early nineties, is an habitue of that foreign country. In his new memoir, *Being Ninety: A Texas Poet's Life*, he also proves to be both an able interpreter and a congenial guide to a place we're all destined to inhabit, if we're fortunate.

Williams, who lives alone in the Texas Panhandle college town of Canyon, describes himself as a Texas poet. He is that— and has been for most of his adult life—but he also has been a record-shop clerk in Denver; a circulation manager in Anaheim; a journalism professor at Baylor; a newspaperman in Amarillo, Fort Worth, and elsewhere; a college journalism professor in South Dakota; a newspaper publisher in Miami (Texas, that is); and a college English instructor in Canyon, as well as a writer of fiction and a classically trained singer (who still sings). He's also translated *Beowulf* from the original Old English and has written a narrative poem, loosely based on that translation, set in 1890s Texas. ("Wolfe," as Williams calls his version, precedes his memoir in this book.)

"Have I mentioned that I'm a grouch?" Williams asks. "Still, I'm healthy, energetic, and probably, except for one thing, as happy as I was at, say, thirty. That one thing, of course, is the grimmest curse of age: the inevitable loss of loved ones." His most painful loss is that of Nell, his wife and beloved companion for sixty-two years.

I've never met Williams, so I can't say how grouchy he really is. What I can say, having read what he calls "this casual chronicle," is that I'd like to join him on his regular walks around his Canyon neighborhood. I'd like to hear him recollect what it was like to be alive during the Depression years, during World War II and on into the decades that I know.

Williams has been good over nine decades of a richly varied life at "absorbing experiences," whether covering the riots that erupted in 1962 at Ole Miss over the admission of a Black man, James Meredith, or describing, good-naturedly, the everyday challenges of old age. For the young and the middle-aged, for those beyond middle age, *Being Ninety* is a welcome gift.

BEING NINETY

I.

I tell myself, these days, that the nineties are as the nineties do. One thing they do in my case is remind me not to whirl around too fast when I hear the grits boiling over. If I forget, I'm likely to lose my balance and stagger halfway across the kitchen. Funny how little space bad balance gets in the chronicles of age. That may be because the chroniclers of age are usually young.

I'm setting out to be an exception. As I write this casual chronicle, I have seventeen months of my nineties to look back on, or seven months of ninety-two to look ahead to—if in fact I live that long, but of course any of us can say that. I hope to reveal, or at least suggest, to young people of, say, thirty, or, say, eighty, how I happened to get here and what it's like here. Not that it will be the same for others when they have hobbled across the border into this last of the two-digit decades. My twenties or eighties were not like theirs, and theirs weren't, or aren't, like anybody else's. Neither, so far, are my nineties like any of my previous decades.

On the very day I began the first of these nine-plus decades, something else was born. It had its start on Wall Street, and its birth name was Black Thursday. The other birthplace, mine, was Abilene, Texas, and the date was October 24, 1929, the day the Great Depression first stirred, though October 29, Black Tuesday, was the day it stood up and gave a catastrophic shrug. My dad worked in sales for Radio Corporation of America, but the job gave out after a couple of years, and for some time we lived in extreme poverty—lived happily for the most part, in my recollection and by my parents' accounts. Still, all I think, say, or write during the present year is bound to reflect, to some degree, the tones and colors of the thirties and of the four years that followed soon afterward. The Great Depression and World War II left antibodies in me that somehow pertain to the present, as did, speaking figuratively because I was never infected, the now-fading COVID plague—I hate the word pandemic, along with a lot of other recently hatched words. A lot of recently hatched ideas, too, and objects. Have I mentioned that I'm a grouch? Still, I'm healthy, energetic, and probably, except for one thing, as happy as I was at, say, thirty. The one thing, of course, is the grimmest curse of age: the inevitable loss of loved ones. My state of reasonable contentment does not suggest that I come nearer to accepting or even understanding much of the thought or many of the activities of people who run the world these days. It's just that I have finally begun to understand that they are not going to do and say things to my liking and that my reaction to their ways—a baffled resentment—is not going to change. Though I have abandoned or considerably modified many of the cruel, backward ideas that I shared with most Texans of my youth, an aftertaste of them lingers despite all my mental mouth washing. I admit that the taste does not always offend me.

It's not as if I had had full exposure to either of the national and world crises of my childhood. My family in the mid-1930s was desperately poor by modern standards, but it was an adventurous, fresh-air style of poverty. We lived in a pair of canvas tents for a while and then in a homemade rock cabin in the South Texas brush country, without electricity, heat, or running water, but we were off to ourselves in pungent countryside, not jammed into grimy rooms in the slums. Our animal neighbors were not packs of scrabbling rats but just the occasional coyote or rattlesnake. And though we once came to within a single meal of hunger, we never got all the way there. The Depression, in my very limited experience, wasn't much like COVID-19, but the two had this in common: their constant presence in the awareness, like a bad-tasting salt lick down in an arroyo of the gray matter. That was the way the thirties affected grown people, at least. I didn't know we were in a depression, though I heard my folks using the word. To a kid in his single digits, what I saw and felt was just the way things were.

The war years, on the other hand, could not pass unrecognized. Every move we made, every thought we entertained, played out above a continuo of war awareness. I was in or nearly in my teens, but I think that even if I had still been a child with unchanged voice I would have been constantly war-aware, like everybody else. We cut back on sugar, on beef, on coffee, on travel, "for the duration." I never heard that phrase in connection with COVID-19, by the way, but it would have fit. No more ball games for the duration, no more hugging for the duration. And underneath everything during COVID, much as in World War II, was the muted thump of a big drum that said death, death, death. At ninety, with the virus all around, my hearing of that thump, though not of much else, was extra-keen. I could mask it by singing "Popeye the Sailor Man" or "An die Musik" while emptying the dishwasher, but it came right back. Could it be that when one is ninety, that drum is going to sound whether or not there is an epidemic?

One thing I have learned from COVID-19 is that death, whenever it comes and from whatever source, will probably not terrify me as it did Schubert's poor maiden. Twice while the infections began stirring, I felt weaker than normal, and once I also had a slightly sore throat. I immediately thought of what I would do, in what order, if this was, as they say, it. I would phone my doctor, then phone each of my two children, then grab the flash drive out of my computer tower and put it in my pocket. I imagined myself in a hospital room, getting probed, gasping for breath, losing consciousness.

Though not charmed by those images, I felt no emotion darker than resignation. What right did I have to be ninety in the first place? I had let myself aim for a hundred, all right, but there were no guarantees, and I knew it. About then I took my temperature, since I had heard that fever was one of the first signs of the virus. It was ninety-six-point-something. Not this time, then. I felt relieved, amused at my imaginings, and, mostly, set to go on with the kind of day COVID-19 had limited me to and granted me. We do what we can do, as long as we can. As we did in the thirties and forties, we tell ourselves we're here and we're lucky. Or maybe the word is blessed.

An activity that may have helped me arrive at my present decade and that certainly helps me enjoy it is an activity allowed and even approved during COVID. It was okay, still, to walk. I have done so, with few exceptions, for roughly an hour a day, six days most weeks, for the twenty-one years since I retired from gainful employment and became solely a writer of poetry and fiction, which, for the great majority of us, is employment of a sort but a long way from gainful. In late May, some afternoons in Canyon, Texas, where I live, are already too hot for pleasant walking. Though I've always hated summer heat, I went ahead all through my eighties and did my walking, or, usually, plodding, in the nearly cloudless evenings along mostly shadeless streets. It was hotter last year than before, thanks probably to most of us who drive, to nearly all of us who heat and cool our houses, and to our millions of cattle and sheep, but thanks also to my diminished tolerance of heat. So, back when I was ninety,

I indulged my intolerance for a while and, on days that promised to be hot, walked before breakfast. Canyon is thirty-five hundred feet above sea level and almost as far north as you can get in Texas. Most summer mornings are somewhere between pleasant and delightful.

On the first day of the early walks, I got up at six-thirty, mumped into my clothes and walking shoes, grimaced through two minutes of squats and knee-lifts, and clumped out the door into the coolness. Immediately I stopped and threw my head back as in my teens, amazed by the almost clutchable fragrance of the air. The east breeze, coming off a prairie field a quarter mile away, was proclaiming clover, daisies, grass, and surely some kind of mint. My sense of smell has always been weak, and age has not strengthened it, but amid those pervasive nectars Methuselah would have shut his eyes and smiled. My joints were feeling their age; my nose was six years old on a dewy morning in the 1930s. How could there be killer virions in that air?

My house is just across the alley from extensive pastures where a small herd of feeder calves often grazes, and though a lot of my walking follows paved streets between look-alike houses, the fields are always close. Toward the end of the outbound part of my walk, where I have left the suburbs for a few minutes and am following a one-lane, hard-packed dirt road around a curve, I sometimes find that the calves have moved from behind my house to the part of the pasture just across a barbed-wire fence from where my walk has taken me. I stop. If the nearest calf sees me walking in its direction, it will stiffen and stare at me in alarm, no doubt remembering how a man in a broad-brimmed hat like mine once burned deeply into its skin with a red-hot iron. Unless I change direction, the calf will quickly turn and flee, joined by all the rest of its fearful, milling kind. I never worked with cattle, never owned a single calf, but I grew up in small-town Texas and had kinfolks, including my dad, who knew the ways of both cattle and ranchers. So I know the certainty that a herd of spooked calves will run off some of the valuable pounds their owner is trying to put on their bones. I turn left, grumbling at animals that have made me miss the nicest part of my walk for the sake of their figures.

On a morning when there were no calves to spook, I walked around the bend of the road and saw a small, dark shape ahead in tall grass and weeds. I stopped to look. An animal, or a trash bag? Then it stirred, and when it raised its head, I saw its white, lengthwise stripe. The animal paid me no mind. After a bit, foraging, it turned around in a graceful, headless and tailless swirl of purest black-and-white, a deep-furred, vivified boa doing a *renversé* from maybe *Swan Lake*. The untaught gracefulness of nature. Beautiful. How unfairly we judge things. A couple of walks later I saw what had to be the same creature out in the open, waddling away from my road about as gracefully as an intoxicated sumo wrestler. How fickle our impressions are.

Those scenes reminded me of the time, fifty years ago, when my wife and I, sleeping with the window open in a different house, in the country near Canyon, were roused by barking just outside and then, instantly, a burst of something more hostile than mere stench, a mephitic eruption that shocked and sickened us. Our Airedale, Alec, had chosen a spot just under the window for his first encounter with one of the skunks that lived out in the bear grass on the slope behind our house. That encounter was enough for him. A day or two later, when we had washed him in tomato juice and he had resumed his old lifestyle, I watched him lie without stirring or protesting as a skunk a few feet away ate Kibbles out of his doggie dish. I could imagine what agonies of Airedale restraint poor Alec was undergoing.

They say that walking is wonderful for the heart. I know it's wonderful for whatever organ it is—not the brain, or not the main brain—that thinks up poetry, and prose, too. Think of Wordsworth's walking poems, and Frost's, and on and on, before them and after them. I often get an idea, usually just an image, on my walks. The trick then is to remember it till I get home and can try to put a poem around it. That is the way most of my poems start: with an image, usually from nature. As for the benefits that walking confers on health and longevity, all I can say is that I've always walked a lot, and here I am.

I do suspect, though, that the main thing I've done to get here was to choose my genes carefully. My dad lived to ninety-five; a sister of his to 102; their maternal granddad to just short of a hundred; a Williams first cousin of mine, female, to the same; one of my mother's sisters to ninety-nine. My brother is ninety-seven. My mother, who died at eighty-eight, had had Alzheimer's disease for ten years. Maybe she would otherwise have made the nineties, too. Genes have to be a large factor in ninetyhood, along with walks, tobaccolessness, not too much alcohol, and maybe having something you still want to write. Given those givens, getting to ninety is simple.

Once there, why, you start each day by getting up. You might as well, you've lain awake for an hour and a half, left side, right side, drawing up a foot to release a vicious cramp in the calf, snuffling so you can breathe through your uphill nostril, trying your left hand, then your right hand, under your pillow, under your cheek, at arm's length out on the cover, telling yourself, "Stay awake. Don't go to sleep," as you've seen suggested online, and hoping each change of position will spring the trapdoor and drop you into the dusky cellar of sleep. Nothing does, and now it's six-thirty. You curse your way out of bed. Careful. Don't start another cramp as you wiggle your feet into your slippers. Stand up, old-cow-on-a-frosty-morning. Is your knee going to hurt like this all day? Who the hell invented up, anyway?

The question, though rhetorical, takes you back to child-hood again, to the Depression days of innocent radio serials—in this case, to *Easy Aces,* in which the stock line with each episode was Jane Ace's indignant, "Who do you think you are? Anyway?" There was a stock line or a stock occurrence in every episode of every program, such as the Great Gildersleeve's laugh, rolling into the bottom of a melodious barrel and out again. Or Fibber McGee's opening of the door to the glutted hall closet in spite of Molly's "No, McGee!" Or Edgar Bergen's exchanges, his mouth no doubt barely moving on the replies, with his wooden protégé, Charlie McCarthy:

"Charlie, don't you know that alcohol is slow poison?"

"Slow poison?"

"Slow poison."

"Slow poison?"

"Slow poison!"

"Well,... I'm in no hurry."

(I quote from memories of eighty-some-odd years ago, not from the YouTube retrievals, which I now lack the patience and possibly the technique to enjoy.)

I was a child; I laughed. But so did my parents. The Great Depression was a simple time. We were easily amused.

A pleasant part of being ninety-plus is remembering those days. But I'm up now, and past radio gives way to present coffee. Remember, I tell myself as I blear around the kitchen: put water in the coffee pot. A few months ago, not long after I had switched from instant coffee to percolator, I plugged the thing in with the basket properly full of coffee and went about my egg and bacon cookery. After a while I realized that I didn't hear the usual snuffling and hiccupping as coffee brewed, and was that smoke I smelled? I unplugged the thing, swearing, and let it cool. I had forgotten to put water in it. While it got hot again, this time properly filled, I ate with my egg and bacon unwashed-down, my drowsiness uncaffeined-up. Stupid, stupid, stupid, I kept saying. And being ninety, I did the same thing twice more in the next couple of weeks. At fifty, I probably would have stopped at two, total. Age doesn't so much cause new stupidities as make the existing ones stupider.

My memory of important things has always been poor, but for unimportant ones—a characterful expression overheard, the shrinking of a friend's pupils at some thoughtless remark I've made—it has been pretty good. A few years ago I sat in the lobby of the county judge's office in Canyon, waiting, and listened to other people's conversations with the receptionist. A farmer, overalled and fairly well up in years, was saying, "I told ol' Flem, I says, 'Flem, I'll tell you what.'" A little later, a middle-aged woman in a dress and heels said, "She had these two little old boys that, I don't know, you just wanted to backhand 'em." Those I will probably remember till I die, but I have long forgotten what I was waiting to see the county judge about. I remember the sound of cannons firing blanks to scare birds away from the vineyards near our house on Long Island, where I was a *Newsday* writer in the late 1980s, but I can't tell you whether we rented or bought our house there, or what kind of car I was driving, or what our living room chairs looked like.

Emptinesses of that kind proliferate at ninety, for me at least. By looking back at an old letter I've kept in my documents file, I see that when I was working for *The Wichita Eagle* twenty-five years ago I spent a few days as a guest writing coach at the *Journal of Commerce* in New York. I have no memory whatsoever of going there, being there, working there. But something I do vividly remember from those days, the 1990s, was finding a morel in one of our flower beds in Wichita. I identified it conclusively with a book I had, and at lunchtime, sautéed in butter, it had the pristinely wonderful taste that only fresh wild things can have. Nell, my wife, though, responsibly declined to try it. In case I had misidentified it, she wanted to be on hand to call the EMTs. If that had happened and I had gone to the hospital and come near to dying, would I now remember that part of the experience? Given the blurrings of age plus my trivia-focused memory, probably not. Only the taste of the morel.

It may be that if I had spent all my career at one place I would remember more of the important things. Doing that, staying, was no more in my genes than dying young was. My dad did not stay, not until he was into his seventh decade. True, his and our frequent moves were often mandated—first by the Civilian Conservation Corps, in whose ranks, in the 1930s and a little beyond, he rose from "educational adviser" to camp commander, and second by the Army, in which, during World War II, he was an officer as he had also been in World War I. My mother, my older brother and younger sister and I followed him almost everywhere he was sent, though not to Guam, where he spent the final months of the war, after we had taken the island back from the Japanese.

Before the CCC, before the war, we went wherever there was a job or the hope of a job. To El Paso and then to Denver and then, like so many other jobless families, to California, and then to Oregon, where Dad had a job trying to sell soap to grocery stores. He hated the job. We were in Portland long enough for Bob, riding his bike down a steep hill in front of our house, to fall and break his collarbone. We must have been doing fairly well financially, for the times, since he did own a bike and we did have a house—a decent one, it seems to me. As usual, though, Dad had a big idea about going into business. He quit the soap-selling job and set out making mayonnaise, to which he gave the brand name Portland Rose. He got as far as accumulating an inventory. He stored it in a basement. It spoiled.

Next: the Oregon coast, where we lived in a tent in the great, damp woods beside the Nestucca River, hoping to homestead as Dad's close friend and my eponym, Don Mace, and his wife were doing. I was only three years old, but I remember the shaky rope bridge we walked to cross the river, and I remember that Cinco, our precocious short-haired fox terrier, fell into the swift current and my big brother, Bob, threw him a coffee can lid as he struggled. He got out on his own. We had neighbors, named, I think, Scheese, not homesteaders but backwoods people who had been there a long time. They were indulgent and helpful to us. One or more of the sons killed two, maybe three, fine mule deer bucks with as many shots—we heard them. They gave us a large store of the wonderful venison, which Mother canned in Mason jars. We must have eaten it for weeks. We went blackberrying in the woods. Possibly we ate trout out of the river—I remember Bob catching a wiggly little one. The woods were, for us kids and for Mother, too, a way of life and place of life that for years afterward seemed Edenic. After a few months, though, my folks gave up on homesteading, at least in part because I, riding my rudimentary tricycle, called a kiddie-car, tipped over onto a wood stove and burned my hand. I remember crying afterward because I wanted Mrs. Scheese, not anybody else, to come and change the dressing. I still have the scar from that burn. My accident reminded my folks of how far it was to a doctor. They left.

Back to California, where my dad tried to sell oranges from a cart and where we were down to one meal's worth of food, not counting the abundant oranges, when the mail brought a disability check from the government, compensation for the disabling of one testicle that mumps had caused Dad when he was in France in 1918. (If the mumps had hit both sides, you would not be reading this.) The check, for several hundred dollars, got us across the Mojave Desert in a faltering car—I remember that it was a Maxwell, but my dad's memoir, *Joyful Trek*, calls it a Buick—with dampened and redampened dish towels hanging in the windows to keep us all, barely, from broiling. On to the vicinity of Uvalde, Texas, where we bought thirty acres of land "for thirty dollars an acre, with nothing down," the memoir says, and pitched two tents in the shade of big live oaks that were bending this way and that, as in a *molto lento* ballet, a hundred years between moves. Dad asked a farmer if he could plant a garden on a little of the farmer's land, which adjoined ours. "Yay betchee," the farmer said. The words, as I can still hear Dad repeating them to me, come close to summing up a warm generosity that throve during the Depression.

What days those were, for a boy of four and five. The live oaks' slants were right for my climbing, the cardinals sang, owls woof-woofed at night, the oak fire gave a tannic warmth that settled into our lungs as if being welcomed home, and the brown-topped, gently stratified biscuits my mother made in a Dutch oven down in the coals would have brought a "Magnifiques!" from any Michelin judge lucky enough to have been sent that way. One night I came almost awake to a loud noise, and the next morning my dad showed us, draped over the bumper of our car, a huge, fat rattlesnake he had shot in the glow of a lantern. I was impressed but not scared. To a kid living in the brush, snakes were routine. To his mother, too, but more about that later.

I still had the kiddie-car that I had tipped over in Oregon, and I pedaled it around on the hard dirt until one morning Dad backed over it. I fussed at him, but when he said, "Son, you shouldn't have left it in the driveway," I saw that he was right. Now, since I've had kids of my own, I can imagine how terrified he was until he piled out of the car and saw that the kiddie-car hadn't been occupied.

It seems to me that most writers who win big prizes, who get on the best-seller lists, who have their books made into movies, have something in common: unhappy childhoods, with one or both parents unloving, brutal, drunk, or absent. Aha, there's my trouble. I had sober, loving, indulgent, and yet firm and sensible parents, and though I underwent bullying in my early schooldays, it wasn't enough to whine about through all my adulthood. No wonder my name is not on every lip, my latest book on every shelf. My mother put up patiently with my supposed illnesses when I was a kid, though she must have been pretty sure that half of them arose from a strong desire to stay home from school and read *Penrod* or *Open Road for Boys*.

My dad tried now and then to teach me how to throw, how to punt, how to tackle. He was superbly coordinated, and such things came easy to him, but he never lost patience at my unteachableness. I don't remember that either of my parents scolded or spanked me when, as a child of four or five, I gave possibly the first indication of my lifelong helplessness in the presence of mechanisms. Wandering about the yard, I found a piece of stiff, heavy wire that was bent at right angles. Like a crank, I thought, and I had seen Dad crank one of the family's string of wretched cars. The one that was parked at the edge of the yard, though, had what a lot of people called a *self*-starter, and so no crank stuck out above the front bumper. I provided one. I jammed the heavy wire here, there, and there, feeling it crunch through the grille each time. The car still wouldn't start. I gave up the game, and it must have been the next day before Dad discovered that the radiator was dry and couldn't be filled. He may have burned up the engine finding out—I don't remember, and now that Bob, my brother, is in a nursing home in Michigan and, at ninety-seven, poor fellow, keeps suggesting that he and I go down to the Hill Country "and see how Pap is doing," there's nobody to ask. I did ask Mother, though, when I was in my middle years, if I really had ruined that car. Yes, she said, I had.

My parents, during the later stages of the Depression, by which time we lived in a real house, bought me a roomful of toys, most of which I played with once and then ignored: a chemistry set, an Erector set, a cowboy suit, a realistic toy six-shooter, a BB pistol that shot tiny pellets harmlessly, a BB rifle that could sting hard and maybe break the skin, marbles, a gyroscope. I did use the roller skates they got me, and, come to think of it, I never had a real football till I was a senior in high school, or a baseball or bat, or a bicycle. I guess I was spoiled the right amount. What have proven to be the best gifts were of course the presences of books, the talk about them, the classical music on the radio and played by my mother on the piano, and the quotations from Khayyám, Browning, Millay, Frost, Kipling around the table. Then there was the love of trees, birds, flowers, mountains, clear streams, fat cattle, and fertile-looking fields of cotton or corn. I plead guilty: the home part of my childhood was happy.

I sometimes ponder my dad's inability to find a job, even in those times. He was energetic, smart, and resourceful, and he had a degree from a small Texas college, plus a graduate semester at Harvard, plus some days, weeks, or months of classes, conducted in French, at the University of Grenoble just after The World War, as we then called it. Maybe it was as he said much later: "I could always sell anything but myself." He was only five-feet-seven and a half—a runt, he called himself, with a trace of shame. But his remarkable quickness had gotten him a position as first-string end on the football team at Simmons College (now Hardin-Simmons University), and when, in his forties or fifties, he ran across an old classmate and introduced himself, the response was, "You mean Whitey Williams, the best fighter in the school?"

That was the character in which he tackled the limitations of camping out. He dug a well by hand, capering and yelling with joy when he struck clear water at twenty feet. He has to have dug a pit and built an outhouse over it, though for some reason I can't recall using it. He went to the library in Uvalde, two miles away, and read up on mortar-making. Then he dug another deep pit, stacked small limestone rocks in it that he had hauled from the bed of the Nueces River, cooked them all night with a wood fire, and the next day dumped them into barrels of cool water, where they exploded into lime. Using that to make mortar to put between more riverbed rocks, he built a one-room house with oilcloth-screened windows and a wood floor. There were of course no electric lights, only kerosene lamps, and no plumbing, no heating or cooling, no radio. But my mother had a kerosene cook stove, and we sat at a wooden table that Dad may well have made and drank wonderful well water out of our blue-enameled metal cups.

Cinco, the little dog, who looked much like the one with his head cocked toward "His Master's Voice" coming out of the big speaker of the RCA Victrola—surely the best trademark ever created—had a cup, too, for his water, and once, at supper, I saw him sit by it and try to pick it up with his paws, the way he had seen us do. The cup fell and spilled, of course. Poor Cinco was as clearly surprised and disappointed as a three-year-old child would have been.

After some months, my dad got a job teaching all six (maybe eight) grades at a one-room school and my mother worked, too, as his assistant. That school was deep in what would have been called the backwoods if the mesquite brush had been taller. I often sat in on the lessons, as I said in a column in *The Wichita Eagle* during the 1990s, when my memory was sharper than it is now:

> —A lot of the kids spoke Spanish, and it was a
> treat when a small chorus of them sang "Rancho
> Grande" to the student body. Another performance
> was by one of the older girls who lived in the
> brush thereabouts. It was close to the Christmas-
> New Year holidays, and she declaimed Tennyson,
> country style: "Rang Out, Wal' Bells." Country was
> really country in those days. I think she was also
> the one who recited something about that soaring
> bird of prey, the iggle.

Do I remember being amused at her style, as young as I was, or is it only that my folks told about it with amusement much later? I do clearly remember her voice, a whangy drone, along with her frightened face and eyes, poor girl.

At recess, I played outside with the older kids. One of them, a boy called Sonny Man, maybe eight years old, climbed a mesquite tree once and slipped. He fell against a limb, climbed down, and went into the building with a nail-like thorn that must have been at least an inch long embedded in his shoulder. "Looks like a elephant stuck his horn in me, Mr. Williams," he said. My dad pulled it out with pliers and put mercurochrome— monkey blood, we called it—on the place. Sonny Man went back outside and finished playing. I don't think he cried. Some of the children spoke Spanish, and they would sometimes sing "La cucaracha." Mother, though she used English well and had a sharp ear for shades of meaning, was not good at foreign languages. ("Making all those faces just doesn't seem ladylike," she told me when I was well grown.) So when the kids sang the last line, about the poor cockroach being unable to travel because he lacked "Marihuana que fumar" (marijuana to smoke), she thought they were looking forward to "Marijuana cake tomorr'."

I was blessed enough—or was it cursed enough?—to have been taught to read by my mother and my big brother, Bob, who was four years older than I and already taking on responsibility not only for my instruction but also for my protection. One day when he and I were rambling in the brush he heard, or imagined he heard, a pack of javelinas, little tusked, piglike animals that could be dangerous. He boosted me up a mesquite tree and then stood guard at the bottom with his pocketknife out and open. No pack came along, but I was stirred by his bravery, not reflecting until years afterward that he could have just climbed the tree, too. His schoolroom for me was outside under the oaks, where we stood as he taught me the sounds of the letters, with attention to special cases such as the short *a* that becomes a long *a* when followed by a single consonant and *e*. My mother had already taught me the ABCs. With those introductions, I could read practically overnight, it seems to me. I read things Mother had already read to me: *A Child's Garden of Verses*, by Robert Louis Stevenson, in which my favorite poem was the one starting, "Dark brown is the river, / Golden is the sand." I loved the gentle imagery of those lines, though I had no idea what was meant in another line by "Castles of the foam." All of us except Dad practically memorized *Winnie-the-Pooh*, by A.A. Milne, about a lovably dumb little bear and his small friend, Christopher Robin, neither of them much like their Disney versions-to-be. There probably wasn't a lot more reading material for me around the cabin, though I may have started on Mark Van Doren's wonderful *An Anthology of World Poetry*, if that was already on hand. My folks did love poetry, including some of the translations in the anthology. My dad told a story about one of his early dates with my mother. She confided to him that she had a favorite poet. "Uh-oh," he thought, "here comes Longfellow." But it was a certain Persian, or what survived of him in Edward FitzGerald's deathless translation of the *Rubáiyát of Omar Khayyám*. Dad loved the poem, too. In the Van Doren anthology, both of my parents memorized and quoted Edwin Arlington Robinson's delicate translation of Sappho's "The Dust of Timas":

> This dust was Timas; and they say
> That almost on her wedding day
> She found her bridal home to be
> The dark house of Persephone.
>
> And many maidens, knowing then
> That she would not come back again,
> Unbound their curls; and all in tears,
> They cut them off with sharpened shears.

Both of them, though, frowned at the anticlimax of the last two words. "Why not 'silver shears'?" Mother suggested. Maybe that would have been too far from the original, but how about "fine-drawn shears"? Afraid my one semester of Greek, fifty years ago, is of no help here.

I must have been allergic to the oaks or to something else around us. I developed a vicious headache, so bad that my folks borrowed the Ford coupé that belonged to my mother's sister and her husband, who lived in Uvalde, and with me curled up in agony on the shelf behind the seat drove to San Antonio to see a doctor. The prescription was a tonsillectomy, which did not solve my problem and I'm pretty sure had nothing to do with it. But I think that once more, as in Oregon, my health and the likely need of good medical care in the future must have been one of the reasons my dad gave in and, against his principles, took the job with Roosevelt's Civilian Conservation Corps—the CCC.

Off, then, to McGregor, a small town near Waco, in Central Texas. I hated it at first, in good part because there were no live oaks near our house, only hackberries, whose straight-up trunks were hard to climb and besides were covered with scaly vertical ridges of bark that marked my legs with white scrapes that shortly turned red. Kids must have closer ties to the apes than grown people do. The absence of good climbing trees was almost as great a lack, to me, as the absence of books to read would have been. One day when I was missing Uvalde badly and no doubt whining about it, my mother comforted me, or meant to do so, by singing, "We will sing one song for the old Uvalde home," whereupon I broke into tears. She was surprised and touched. I still almost cry when I hear a sad song, even a not quite serious or at least not quite sober one such as "Show me the way to go home."

The thought of Uvalde still moves me, too, and so much so that a few years ago, when my brother, Bob, was visiting, we drove five hundred miles to get there, went two miles southeast of town on the Batesville road, and by golly, to our right, not far back from the road, was a leaning live oak that had to be the one, back in the thirties, that I loved the most and spent many of my happiest hours in. There was a rock house in the right place, too, though much bigger and better-finished than the one my dad had built. I knocked on the door, told the owner why I was there, and, with his permission, stiffly and precariously climbed the dear old oak once again. Then the owner took us to the back of the house and showed us a patch of stonework that was less finished than the rest. It came out of the old cabin, he said.

So after eighty years I had found the way to go home. No, just to one place that had been home. Other places, much later, came to be home, too. What all of them lack, now, is the people that made them what they were: my mother and dad, my grand-dad, my aunts, and, most of all, Nell, who made us wonderful homes out of place after place and to whom I was married for sixty-two years before her death in late 2018. That is the worst thing about being ninety. There is no way to go home. Home was people.

I came to like a lot of things about McGregor, but school was not one of them. I was easily reading *The Adventures of Tom Sawyer*, along with the awful Big Little Books, the Sappho translations and Keats odes in the Van Doren poetry anthology, Popeye and "The Katzenjammer Kids" and "Andy Gump" in the funnies, and, over and over again, bits of *The Book of Knowl-edge*. When I was in my sixties and still had my childhood set of that remarkable twenty-volume encyclopedia, I wrote a column about it for *The Wichita Eagle*, where I worked. One reason the set was so appealing, I said, was

—the warm, gentle style, directed at kids but not condescending. As a matter of fact, how many kids today would make much sense of the statement, in one typical story, about the English sailors who boarded a French ship "with such impetuosity that the enemy was filled with consternation and dismay"?

The set was organized in short segments, the subjects including The Book of Plant Life, The Book of Literature, The Book of Fine Arts, and The Book of Wonder, which answered the questions "Could we walk without our toes?" and "Why does a match strike?" When I was little, I read the answers to those, but in general I did a lot more looking at the pictures than reading the text. There was a large exception, as I said in an *Eagle* column:

—It was *The Book of Knowledge* that first drew me to grown-up poetry. Some of the stuff it printed was second-rate Victorian sermonizing, and I rightly skipped it. But I read and reread the Burns and Tennyson poems.... An introductory note says that the premise behind the division into short, recurring sections, rather than devoting a volume each to animals, plants and so on, was that "the average child cannot concentrate long upon those subjects which require close attention." Remember, there was no television to blame that on. My willingness to concentrate, when I was a kid, was too small even for the format of *The Book of Knowledge*. But if I had read the twenty volumes straight through, I would have acquired the essentials of a fine education.

Because I skipped the first grade in McGregor and took the next two grades in one year, I was three years younger than my classmates all the way through grammar school, junior high, and high school. I was shy anyway, and awkward, and grammatical. I therefore got bullied, and probably enough that, these days, the authorities would be called in. I didn't like it, of course, but I don't remember thinking it was unfair. It was just life, like the Depression. I doubt that the big boys knew my age. I certainly didn't tell them; I was ashamed of it.

As for the little girls, I didn't let their great maturity discourage my attentions. I fell in love with Mary Mae, and Cledyth, and especially with a small, pretty, brown-eyed girl named Doris. One day, between classes, I scrawled "Don + Doris" in a heart on a piece of tablet paper and handed it to her. She read the note and then chased me all around the room, hitting me on the head with it. After school one day, when I was walking home with a neighbor kid, Bruce, I looked back and saw Jimmy Jenkins, a classmate, walking in the same direction with a girl. Doris! They hadn't noticed us; we hid in a shed next to the sidewalk. I told Bruce that when they got to the shed I would call Jimmy a sissy, and then, when we were fighting, would yell for help. Agreed. Bruce was even younger than I, but the two of us might be able to teach Jimmy a lesson, I thought.

When Jimmy and Doris came along, I stuck my head out and said the deadly word. Doris, unasked, held out her hands for Jimmy's books, and he, without a word, lit into me. I tried to fight back. No use. I was helpless, smothered in volleys of lefts and rights. I don't think I was knocked down, but I must have cried. Something, at least, signaled that the fight was over. Jimmy retrieved his books and walked on with Doris.

"Why didn't you come and help?" I said to Bruce, snuffling.

"You never called me," he said.

"I couldn't. I was getting beat up too bad." I was laughing by then, ruefully.

My reading at home amounted to the most lasting and influential part of my education, but I learned valuable things in school, too. It was in the fourth grade, I think, that my teacher—I wish I could remember her name—drilled us day after day in parts of speech and verb conjugations. A noun is the name of a person, place, or thing. An adjective modifies a noun. Do, did, done. Go, went, gone. Lie, lay, lain. Lay, laid, laid. We recited them together, teacher and class, over and over. I wonder if any of the kids in that class grew up to say, "I was laying there," as most of their parents said, as at least fifty percent of Americans and eighty percent of Texans now do. We learned about Admiral Byrd and the North Pole, we memorized "The Star-Spangled Banner" and our awful state song, "Texas, Our Texas," and of course we were told, in all seriousness, about little George Washington and his father's cherry tree. We took a field trip to the family farm of a boy named Roland and watched the shearers pull the woolly pelts off sheep's bodies like peeling back thick, smelly carpets.

The thing I liked most about McGregor was spring. It arrived green and dewy, unlike the thorny, year-round dryness of Southwest Texas. Flowers were everywhere—phlox, winecups, daisies, red clover, buttercups full of yellow pollen that you smeared onto a boy's nose and face if he fell for your "Smell this." Bluebonnets, the state flower, covered road banks and open fields with a blue that was deepened by the pure-white sail at the top of each blossom and the barely visible fleck of Bordeaux red on the base of each petal. They are one of the world's great shows of springtime color, comparable to California's golden poppies on their own merits and made still more beautiful by the bursts of "Indian" paintbrush that usually live next to them.

In April of 2019 I went to a poetry gathering in the same general part of Texas and experienced once again the flower array that changed exquisitely day by day and the bird songs everywhere, the cardinals singing CHIP-per chipper chipper chipper chipper and alternately TEE-oo WHIT, WHIT, WHIT,

WHIT, WHIT as they had done in 1936 and in the same Nellie Melba tones, and the mockingbirds perching at the highest, most visible peak of every second tree, quivering and jumping with look-at-me fervor, never taking a breath but exulting in that erotic season with unpunctuated strings of rasps, flutes, squalls, and sweet fragments of impromptu requiems: Texan birds, first shouting down, and then competing melodiously with, all imputations of nightingale or lark. I was six years old again, and spring, again, would never end.

For the times, and for eighteen dollars' rent a month, our house in McGregor was pleasant. It was white-frame, had three bedrooms and of course only one bath, and had gas space heaters for the chilly winters, though not even evaporative coolers for the summers, which were just as miserably hot as those in all of Texas were except in the high altitudes of the Panhandle and the far west. We soon provided the house also with a burly, black, used Steinway upright piano that sounded almost like a concert grand in spite of having a cracked soundboard. Mother often woke us up playing Chopin nocturnes on it. My dad planted a big garden. He knew how to make things grow. I remember potatoes, Kentucky Wonder beans, and radishes.

There was a fine orchard, with peaches, plums, grapes, and fat, bready figs. In the first year or so, before Mother had an electric refrigerator, she made ice cream in a hand-cranked freezer, using peaches newly gathered from the orchard and thick cream scooped off the tops of bottles of unhomogenized milk. When you ate it, your spoon uncovered delicious strings of golden peach. After we got an electric refrigerator, the peach ice cream wasn't quite heavenly anymore, only wonderful. I don't know what brand our refrigerator was, but Frigidaire was what most people called all of its kind, regardless of the makers. The air was full of words like that, that we no longer use. For my brother's ninety-second birthday, a few years ago, I recalled some of them:

I ask you, Bob, where have they gone,
The words we knew, back in the dawn
And maybe dusk, too, of our era?
I want to see if they'll come nearer
In more or less iambic couplets.
Here goes, then: the Dionne quintuplets;
The church key, croup, and BVDs;
Speakeasies, doughboys, S.O.P.s;
Boob meaning dummy and no whit
The rhyming word that wasn't writ
Back then, and hardly ever said,
Not in "mixed company"; car shed;
The funny papers; pizza *pie*;
"Check your tires?" and the pink eye;
Hot tamales; four-on-the-floor;
The counterpane; the sixty-four-
Dollar question; the old-age-pensioned,
Or, hell, old age itself, so mentioned;
The milch cow, thus spelled by the rule;
The teacher's paddle in grade school,
Or grammar school, we said back then
When grammar was still offered in
The public schools. Back then, back there,
The icebox turned to Frigidaire,
You might still have a Gramophone,
Victrolas, though, were better known.
We had a gas stove for the cold,
We said dadblast it, pure-d-old,
For garden seeds, and don't sit there
With your teeth in your mouth. The lodging where
You stayed on trips was a tourist camp.
If you owned a flivver you weren't a tramp.
Icemen and milkmen came around,

Single mothers did not abound,
Or if they did, stayed out of sight.
Oh, there is more that I could write,
But you by now will have thought back
To it and past. Such is the track
Our minds retrace, the more the older,
As if they warmed and not got colder.
I'll end by saying pooey to you
From me, and happy ninety-two.

I've translated the ending couplet here from the original Morse code. The "pooey" line was from the Popeye comic strip. Bob and I regularly sent the phrase to each other, one of us in the garage, the other in the bedroom we shared, with the telegraphy set he had put together, using one or two B batteries and wires. We both learned Morse because our dad had been a radio operator in the World War, and, later, on merchant ships. I can still send code as fast as my fingers will move, though I'm weak on numerals and never learned more than two or three Morse punctuation marks.

For part of our two-and-a-half-years in McGregor, my aunt, Estelle Montgomery, stayed with us and helped Mother, her sister, through her pregnancy with Linda, my sister. Nanty, as my brother and I called her, was single, rather beautiful, an even better cook than Mother, and, as I was told in my middle age, a sad figure, so single-minded in love that after her first and only romance ended, that was it; she would have no more. When Nanty was not with us, we had a maid, a black woman named Rose, very agreeable, very helpful, and with a speaking voice as mellow as Marian Anderson's. Rose had a son, Booker T., of about my age. Sometimes he came to the house with her, and he and I would play. He never went to my school, of course, and I lost track of him when Rose had stopped working for us.

My parents, like everybody we knew, practiced and professed segregation. It was the natural way, we thought. Neither of my folks would have been rude to a black person because of the person's color, and Dad told us children not to use the word that is now written as n—. The alternatives weren't much better. My dad tried sometimes to say Nee-gro, but that just didn't sound like English to him or to us. At the table once, Dad said to me, "Don! Don't eat like a little pickaninny!" Instantly he realized that we were not alone. "I'm *sorry*, Rose," he said, stumbling all over himself, and she replied in her sunny tones, "That's all right, Mr. Williams."

Once, Rose told Mother that her grandmother was very sick. Rose had taken her to the doctor in McGregor, who of course was white. He refused to see her.

"We'd rather be with our own kind, the same as you," Rose said, "but it's not right when they won't treat a poor old lady." Mother agreed, sadly. I'm sure she was torn; she had been brought up by a father who was born in Texas during Reconstruction and whose father was a wounded Confederate veteran of the Civil War. To her, even in the 1930s, Grant was a villain and Lee a hero.

II.

Hackberries were bad enough. The next place the CCC sent us, Memphis, Texas, had very few trees of any kind. It was, and is, in the Panhandle, like Canyon, but much lower in altitude and therefore much hotter in summer. One day when I was, as often, sick or malingering—even I couldn't always be sure which was the case—it was 114 degrees, and Mother put me on a cot in the pointillistic shade of our small locust tree. No help; at 114, nothing helps short of air-conditioning, which we scarcely knew existed. Think of my poor mother, inside and cooking on that day. Our two years in Memphis came at the tail end of the Dust Bowl, too. The tail still had some whip in it. One day, when I was walking the mile northward home from school, I saw a menacing, towering mass that covered the whole sky to the west and was bearing down on our house like a darker, redder embodiment of a "severe weather" warning on today's TV. I started running but wasn't fast enough. I bent, struggling, into the mass and with grit in my teeth ducked through the front door, which was fortunately on the east side of the house.

That was the storm that left sand drifts over the top strands of barbed-wire fences and put dry deltas of sand on the sills of our closed windows. People called such storms dusters, and the books describe them as black, but what I clearly recall is sandstorms, and the sand was red. Still, our location much more often meant clear, pleasant days and cool summer nights. Bob and I spent those nights on cots in the backyard, watching the stars that were the special attractions of dry air and a lack of street-lights. Bob taught me the names of a few constellations, and we often saw "falling stars."

The weather in Memphis made a larger impression on me than the Depression ever did, and that, too, was a long way from over. I had playmates to whom "light bread," meaning the taste-less, gummy, thin-crusted white kind in the grocery store, was a luxury, just because it was bought rather than kneaded and home-baked. Still, there were those beautiful days, and there were good times. We used to drive into the country, squeeze through a barbed-wire fence, and walk in the evening breeze on a brown little knob we called Our Hill. It was really Somebody Else's Hill, but we didn't know whose, and his house, anyway, was out of sight, and besides he wouldn't have minded.

At what most people, to my displeasure, called "the CC camp," my dad was known as "P'fessor." I never attended any of his classes, but I think he taught those mostly unlettered young men the kind of fundamental English structure that I had learned in McGregor and also the elements of mathematics and science, which he was far better at than I have ever been. He told us about asking his class, "What's twice as cold as zero?" One young man, who must have experienced Panhandle win-ters, had the answer: "Zero with the wind blowing." I don't recall that actual combination there, but I remember very well what the weather was like another time when I was walking, or rather, running, home from school. It was on April 6, 1938. At lunchtime that day I had walked the half-mile from the gram-mar school to a brown little wooden store across the street from Memphis High School to buy a fried pie, probably pecan. There was a blustery wind, but that was nothing out of the ordinary. Forecasts back then must have been sketchy, or ignored, or both; I was wearing nothing warmer than a light jacket and didn't need even that as I walked back to school, eating the pie.

But when the bell rang three hours later, I stepped out into a blizzard and a north wind that pummeled my face and chest with snowflakes like the fists of several dozen Jimmy Jenkinses. I ran across the street and ducked behind a house to warm up, and then, freezing, fighting my way forward against the wind, ran two houses north again, sheltering for a minute or so, and onward two houses at a time all the way home. When I finally got there, Mother was waiting at the door with a heated blanket to wrap around me. The next day, snowdrifts covered the top wires on barbed-wire fences the way sand drifts had.

I've looked up that storm. I don't know about Memphis specifically, but at Pampa, north of there, the wind blew at a sustained seventy-seven miles an hour and drifts were ten to twenty feet high. Near there, the same storm buried two rhesus monkeys, Tarzan and Tater, that were the cherished pets of Nell's Uncle Henry, a rancher. They were outside in a cage with the wooden top shut, as Henry had left them while he went into town for some supplies. By the time he had fought his way back home in his pickup, the cage was hidden under a huge drift. He shoveled the snow off and, full of dread, opened the lid. In the cage, perfectly healthy, were not two but three rhesus monkeys. Tater had picked a memorable time to become a mother.

Even in a slow car on poor roads, the Rocky Mountains in New Mexico were an easy drive from Memphis. We went there for at least one summer vacation, staying in our tent near the banks of the rushing Cimarron River, which was as unlike the sandy, trickling Red River near Memphis as anything called a river could possibly be. The grass was soft and damp, the delicate aspen leaves quivered above trunks as white as bluebonnet sails, and the midsummer breeze was October-cool. It was late afternoon. Bob and I told the folks we were going to climb the wooded hill that rose from the river. We would be back by suppertime. Up we went. There was the top, an easy climb. But no, when we got there, there was another top. Then another, and on and on we went until either hunger or the approaching dusk finally made us head back down. We never got to the top. At the tent, our mother and dad were just short of frantic—were about to get a search started, they told us. Kids have no sense. And in the mountains, as I was later reminded many a time on many a slope, it's always a longer way to the top than you think. Too long a way, now. With great effort, I might get up there, and I might still be there. Coming down is much harder on ninety-two-year-old knees than climbing.

At home, we had two nanny goats for a while. I was, I'm afraid, a frail and sickly child, and someone, maybe a doctor, suggested that goats' milk would be better for me than cows'. The providers were a sweet-natured white Saanen and a malignant Nubian, patterned like a pinto horse. We called them the white nanny and the paint nanny. Poor Bob, who was given nearly all the spare jobs around the place because he was strong, capable, and more or less willing, took care of the goats and milked them. The paint nanny had all the malice the other one lacked, and she took it out on poor Bob, butting, balking, and uttering her ungoatlike, rebellious mump-mump-mumps, puffing out her cheeks in threat.

One night she was bawling like a caprine beagle, endlessly. Our bedroom was on the side near the goat pen. We couldn't sleep with that noise. Exasperated, Bob finally went to see what was wrong. When he opened the gate and stepped in, the paint nanny reared up and came down at him with her two front feet, trying to lay him open. Bob had stepped back just in time. Her sharp little hooves slit his pajamas cleanly from top to bottom without touching him. He touched her, though, hard, repeatedly, and with a handy board. She did not reform. I doubt that goat milk improved my health, anyway, and we got rid of both of the wherewithals before many months.

I haven't mentioned religion. In McGregor, the Methodist preacher had made me a member by sprinkling water on my head. Mother, like her father, had been brought up in that church. In her middle age, influenced by Dad's reasoning, she laid aside the basic beliefs of Christianity, though still believing, as he did, in a supreme power. I had come, uninstructed, to think the same way by my late teens or early twenties.

But in Memphis, when I was eight, I had an experience that has kept my belief alive ever since. Our Boston terrier, Cricket, had an angry red sore the size of a blueberry between the lids of his right eye. It refused to go away, and Mother said the vet would have to cut it out. Envisioning a horribly painful, unanesthetized procedure, I went into the shed one day, knelt amid the oblong bales of alfalfa hay, and for probably twenty minutes prayed intensely for God to dissolve the sore. When I had brushed away the bits of hay and gone back into the house, we were getting ready to drive somewhere, all of us. As we got into the car, the dog came wagging up, hoping for a ride.

"Well, *look* at Cricket's eye!" Mother said.

I looked quickly, nodded, and looked away. No surprise to me, the sore was gone. But I said nothing about the reason. It embarrassed me; prayer was a private thing. The sore came back in a day or so, and the vet did remove it—with anesthesia—but I have never doubted that it had vanished for the moment because of my prayer. Was it God's sign to me, though, or had my pleading sent out some kind of curative mind rays? The former, I believe, but either way, it was a remarkable event. I wish I had told my folks, then or ever. The account would have strengthened them in their own belief. But no. Embarrassment, again; damn me for that. I still pray every night but talking about it would be like using the toilet in public. Writing about it is easier, a little.

Regrets like that build up over the decades. Why did I never tell Mother I loved her? I told Nell that, many, many times, but even so I never quite expressed to her my profound gratitude for her selfless, uncomplaining assumption of daily chores, of bookkeeping, of dealing with our recurrent moves, of working all day in uncooled Texas kitchens when we were young while I sat in air-conditioned newsrooms. If there is an afterlife, I intend to spend eternity thanking her. Or will I, will we, remember anything from this life? If not, what's the point of having more? One good thing: if death is all, at least we won't *know* we'll never know the answer to our lives' one big question. Our curiosity won't be disappointed.

Surely Mother knew, though without being told, that I loved her. I did tell Dad. He was in the veterans' hospital at Kerrville, Texas, ninety-five and fading fast but still able to talk a little. "I love you," he said with an effort that, I'm sure, came from more than his weakened condition. We just weren't the kind to say such things. I did, though; I told him I loved him, too. "I know you do," he said, and those were close to the last words he ever said to me. Like me, he found it far easier to express his private self in writing than in speech, and his memoir, *Joyful Trek*, does some of that, along with vivid accounts of his many adventures as soldier, sailor, reporter, inventor, and, finally, rancher, though only on a small, recreational level, amid the oaks and clear streams of the Texas Hill Country. He and Mother had two beautiful decades there before her mental decline began. During those good years she told me she had found a deep sense of contentment in old age.

I'm sure my dad had not found that. He was too restless, too busy wrestling with inventions that did not want to be invented. He won a good many of those matches. He had twenty-four patents. For more than a year, he struggled with the problem of sealing a rotary engine. I believe he finally conceded, as a world of engineers before him had done, that there wasn't a way to win that one. One of his earlier experiments had succeeded in a big way, though. He had invented a mailing machine and sold it to

Dashieu Business Machines for $150,000, and that was how he and Mother, in 1960, could afford to move back to Texas after a decade in Southern California.

Dad's engineering genes skipped me entirely, and so did his roundedness genes. He was at least as good a writer as he was an engineer and inventor. Among his various jobs, three were as a reporter or rewriteman on large newspapers in Dallas, Boston, and Denver. Those jobs both required and taught competent, straightforward writing. "Don't say, 'He attempted to accomplish the difficult matters,'" Dad used to tell me, "Say, 'He tried to do the hard things.'" In *Joyful Trek*, written so late in his life that he never got to hold a copy of the published book, the style does full justice to his restless and adventurous life and also to his poetic perceptions of nature and musings about existence.

When I looked at a passage in it the other day, I realized that this memoir and everything else I had ever written showed that I had his style in my ear. Maybe genes figure there, too. But his adventurer genes passed me by. I have lived a quiet life, and my only excuse for telling you about it is that all my life has had a part in my way of being ninety. And *that*—being ninety–is an adventure that hasn't come out in many books. I think most writers my age figure they've done their work and now they're going to damn well sit by the fire and let the royalties roll in. Ha.

Aside from the dusters and blizzards, which, really, were infrequent, and the episode of Cricket's sore eye, Memphis hasn't left me with much to tell. I for some reason wasn't bullied in school there, and I don't remember falling in love. After all, before we left Memphis the girls in my grade were entering puberty and I was a little boy of ten. Everybody, it seemed to me, was older than I, and that perception stayed with me until, suddenly, a few years ago, everybody became younger than I. I still haven't adjusted. Women my age or near it seem like my grandmothers. The white-bearded pastor of the Presbyterian church in Canyon, a man in his late fifties, strikes me as a patriarch. I belong to that church. Nell was brought up as a Baptist, and I became a Sunday sleeper-in, except for the good many years when I was a choir member and occasional soloist in churches of various denominations in various towns and cities.

Starting in the late 1980s on Long Island, we compromised on the Presbyterians because of their dignified service and serious music. The sermons in Canyon, each of them a tightly constructed, quietly exhortative essay built on biblical examples, usually leave me feeling purified, even a little bit devout, in spite of my long-held reservations. During COVID-19, of course, I only read the texts that the pastor sent around by e-mail. I could also have heard and seen him if I were willing to tinker with Zoom, but virtual, to me, meant and still means what we in the war called ersatz: artificial, unreal. Now back in church, and safely so, so far, I again enjoy the choir and organ, the live sermons, and the faces of people most of whom I see only in church but whose greetings and smiles warm the day for me.

Next move: to the CCC camp a hundred miles to the southwest, near Lubbock. Big embarrassment. On the first day of school, in my junior high class, I somehow let the kid next to me know my age. He immediately started waving his hand, bursting to tell the class my secret. I grabbed his arm and tried to wrestle it down. The teacher, Mr. Cox, scolded me. Was that the way students acted in Memphis?

"Well," I yelled, almost crying, "he was going to tell that I was ten years old, and I didn't want him to."

The secret-teller was laughing. "*You* told him," he said.

In Lubbock, my big brother joined Troop 8 of the Boy Scouts. The scoutmaster had reportedly lived with Indians and so was called Chief. It was not he, though, but the senior Scouts, fifteen to seventeen years old, who inspired hero worship in me. I begged God to let me someday be like them—strong, good-humored, indulgent, brave. They quickly accepted Bob, who was always good at making friends, and I, tagging along, saw a lot of them. They even let me go camping with them. One winter night we were all in pup tents, freezing in our kapok sleeping bags. One of the big boys, Jerry Crawford, who to me was the greatest hero in the bunch, announced after a while that he was moving out into the open. "I want to get the benefit of the moon," he said. All of us laughed long and loud in shiver-driven laughs. Jerry gave up on the moon before long and went back into his tent.

My admiration of him and one or two others was part of growing up but may also have been an inherited tendency. Dad told me once, as if confessing, "I was a hero worshipper," and it was as such that he had chosen a name for me. One of his friends, a witty, urbane fellow whom he had known since college and whose example had drawn him with his family to the Oregon woods, was named Don Mace. Especially as a writer, I'm grateful for the middle name. There are countless Don Williamses around, but I have never run across another Donald Mace Williams, whether a writer or a normal person.

The CCC sent us from Lubbock to Denton, Texas, near Dallas, where Dad was commander of the camp. He was proud of the fact that in each of his three months there, the camp won the district's pennant for general excellence, something it had never won before. But we didn't stay long, even for us. On the recommendation of Don Mace, Dad was hired as editor of *Happy Days*, a weekly paper published in Washington, D.C., covering news of interest to CCC camps. Another short stay. It had looked like a long one, for us, and we had bought a nice, for us, house in a muddy new development in Maryland.

I was a freshman in high school, finding out that Texans and Texas were material for not entirely good humored wisecracks. The other kids thought I talked funny; I thought they did. They said they lived in a "hewse" (like "heh-ose"). I told Mother that when one got hurt he said "Ewch." I also told her about a strange thing other boys called each other: "You queer." I think she wanted to keep me innocent; she nodded and didn't explain. I used the epithet once, luckily on a friend, a cross-eyed kid. He could tell that I didn't know what the word meant. "Queer around the eyes," he said. A nice kid.

My only sharp memories of our stay near D.C. otherwise are of climbing the Washington Monument, of smelling rotting apples on the ground, and of mud, mud, mud. I had a paper route, throwing what must have been *The Washington Post* to houses in our development and often getting bawled out by some subscriber I had missed the day before—my laziness about studying in school carried over to memorizing my list of subscribers. When Pearl Harbor came along, Dad joined the Army Air Corps and, as a captain in S-2 (intelligence), was sent to Miami Beach, Florida. We followed him, except that Bob went back to Lubbock and enrolled in Texas Tech as an engineering major.

For a year or two, I had been practically obsessed with fishing. Did I enjoy Florida! I cast lures or dangled bait in the salt-water canals every day, catching and releasing mostly the dark-meated, strong-tasting but hard-fighting jack crevalles. At school, I enjoyed my first course in Spanish, partly because of Miss Dupree, the teacher, who was small and cute. I was not quite thirteen but already on the way to being a baritone, with, accordingly, the stirrings that would torment me for the rest of my schooldays. Girls in my classes were, of course, much older than I. It wouldn't have mattered much if they hadn't been, I was so awkward and unsure. Still, I looked older than I was. Once or twice, a girl smiled at me with a show of interest—not openly reciprocated, of course.

My hair was as blond as Dad's had been, and one of my classmates in Miami Beach introduced me to another as "my pure Aryan friend." Surprising that a Jewish boy could joke that way, at that time. When Dad was transferred, in February 1943, to a base at Harrisburg, Pennsylvania, he drove us to northern Florida, where he was to catch a train. He and Mother kissed desperately when we left him. For all they knew, it would be their last kiss. She started driving westward—we were going to Lubbock to join Bob—and nearly hit another car, then another. "Look out," I said, helpfully. Then I realized what was wrong. She was crying so hard she could barely see. It was a bad trip—Mother miserably sick, I too timid to do what she told me and go and ask the wife of the motel operator in Alabama or Mississippi to come and stay with her—one of my guilty memories of that generally sorry time of my life.

III.

This chronicle of my moves has placed me only in my early teens, and what has it shown about being ninety? Mainly, I think, that after those moves and many, many others I have finally settled down, body, mind, and soul. Canyon, the plains, my empty house, and even, now, my constant longing for the days when it wasn't empty—those are home, at last. Home is where, twenty-one years ago, I got down to the writing I had been too lazy and conflicted to do for the six decades before. Home is what Nell and I contemplated when, on our retirement, she told me, "I can't think of anyone I'd rather grow old with." I told her neither could I, and we spent some of our happiest years growing old together on the Texas plains where she was born and where she and I met. Illness and pain beset her more and more, but at least we were together. Then, finally, inevitably, we weren't. I've never seriously considered moving, though. Being ninety-two and alone at home is still being, with reservations, at home.

It is also being aware that on those terms home isn't what it used to be. Being ninety-plus, I have nightly leg cramps that potassium pills and a daily banana haven't helped. I have bad hearing. When the pastor in his sermon ad-libs, deadpan, I never know what the congregation is laughing about. In a restaurant, where music is playing or people at other tables are talking or laughing loudly, I can't be sure whether my companion has asked the waiter about the duck or the elk. I have a sore knee from an accident a few years ago, and now the other knee is emulating it, unaided. Pain in the lower back makes me slump until I remember that that's what old men do, and I straighten up, grimacing. (When I was an adolescent, Dad used to tell me, "Stand up straight," and he did so himself, even in his nineties and with a back that I know hurt more than mine does.) The worst thing, though, is that with Nell gone I have had to be ninety on my own. I do my best. Lately, that best has been much augmented by a close relationship with a woman in Austin, five hundred miles away. We manage to see each other fairly often, and between visits we keep in touch daily via e-mail. She has brightened and blessed my nineties.

If I thought I was worse off than other nonagenarians, there would be no point in writing this memoir. I think I'm much better off than most. I can take and enjoy a two-and-a-half to three-mile, moderately fast walk most days among the calves and skunks and mockingbirds. In spite of my trouble understanding spoken words, I can listen with great pleasure to Mozart's third-from-last symphony on the radio. I can enjoy crab cakes, even though they were cooked by me. My memory has slipped, but it never was good, and usually I realize in a day or so that the name I just couldn't remember, that of my neighbor two houses down, has popped into my mind unannounced, like e-mail. I do not feel any age in particular when I talk on the phone or compose e-mail or wave at a masked friend in the grocery store. I'm just myself, the one I've always been. Maybe that will change. For now, I'm in my nineties, and I intend to make the most of it.

People of whatever age have become themselves in good part by absorbing experience. Since one of the experiences I have absorbed was a war, though from a distance, I may have been a little better suited to life in a pandemic than younger people. I remember the constant awareness that "There's a war on." We didn't have to quarantine ourselves, of course, but our consciousness of impermanency and also of danger was pandemic, and it lasted much longer than COVID seems to have done. Will another COVID come along, or the latest one return in force? If so, I'll feel sorry for younger people but will not suffer unbearably on my own.

War memory helps. Honestly, though, the things that help the most are that I'm (1) solitary by nature and (2) a writer. I had for years seen my creative impulse flickering and had finally come to think that a small poem every two or three months was all that remained in me. The plague gave me as a writer the uninterrupted time that had, unbeknownst to me, been a more important lack than that of my erstwhile fervor. I sit down with an idea after supper knowing I can work on it till morning if need be. Sometimes I do. And there's this—this thing that I'm writing, as long as I can keep putting aside the thought that nobody wants to read a memoir by an unknown writer. I try to tell myself, when I have that thought, that this is a memoir by an unknown *ninety-plus-year-old* writer. Everybody wants to read that. Sure, sure.

Solitude comes in various forms. I was alone in the house, nights and parts of days, for Nell's last three months, when she was in a nursing home. Still, I saw her every day, kissed her on arrival and departure, told her I loved her, cut up her lunch for her and helped her eat it, helped her in the bathroom, and otherwise mostly sat in her room and translated Rilke poems while she slept a medicated sleep. After she died, the empty house made itself emptier. Once in a while, though, friends came, or my daughter from her home in Massachusetts, or my son and his wife and children from theirs in Houston—and now, thank God, my new attachment from Austin, my girlfriend. When Nell died, it was still more than a year till COVID, and I drove sixteen miles to Amarillo twice a week for lunch and errands. I went there also for chamber music concerts, for the Amarillo Opera, and for the monthly recitals of Beethoven piano sonatas at Amarillo College. The house was altogether as empty as before when I got home from any of those and heard myself push the door shut behind me, but at least I had had a break.

Then the plague came. I left home only for my walks and for a masked trip to the grocery store when it had just opened on Monday mornings and not many other shoppers were there. My companions were books and magazines, writing, TV and computer news, TV weather, FM classical music all day, e-mail, weekly phone talks with my children, and crossword puzzles in the newspaper on the infrequent days when the clues were more interesting than "___ Vegas." I kept myself company also by such imaginative activities as cooking, eating, dishwashing, trash-taking-out, shaving, and showering. In other words I was, and had to be, a near-hermit. That was no different from millions of others, except that I knew that at my age a COVID-19 infection would be an arm-wrestling match with Death, and so I probably stayed in an emptier house than most.

Emptiness meant without Nell. It therefore meant trauma. I had PTSD, the P standing for Present instead of Post. The disorder unclothed my nerves. I yelled and cursed if I dropped a Frito on the floor. I screamed "Shut up" at the FM people who begged for pledges instead of playing music. When I saw a picture of a cute child or a winsome dog I smiled as instantly and broadly as if they were my own and real—and the apparent end of the plague hasn't changed that reaction. The plague, in fact, has made permanent changes in me, as surely in millions of other people. Sad, sentimental songs—"Danny Boy," "Long Time Ago"—filled then, and still fill, my eyes with tears and my chest with a dark certainty that all is lost, that nothing will return, that I am "a motherless child, a long way from home." I chuckle out loud, still, at poor gag lines in the funnies. I avoid reading accounts of torture or loss. In every way, my middle ground has gone, my balance. So far, I think I haven't, so to speak, fallen, but will I know if I do? Will I lie in a facility, calling my pretty nurse Granddad? Or will I keep on observing my own mental totters as if I were the nurse, saying, aha, old fellow, you nearly lost it there? And probably writing about the experience?

I was saying that we—Mother, my younger sister Linda, and I—were on the way once again to Lubbock. We arrived in time for me to finish three months of the school year. It was also in time, with not much to spare, to see a little more of Bob. Those were the last and best of his Boy Scout years, and he was within one merit badge of his Eagle when, in mid-May, he turned eighteen and immediately went into the Army Air Corps and away. Having no further inducement to stay in Lubbock, we spent the summer in Boise, Idaho, near where Dad was stationed, then moved to Austin, where Mother's father and stepmother lived.

It was the early fall of 1943. I was thirteen and a junior in my fourth high school. I did well in Spanish and English, as always, and got through first-year algebra and plane geometry without great difficulty, since they were easy enough not to require real concentration. Up till then, I had coasted through all subjects, mainly on my reading ability, seldom having to buckle down and study. But though I didn't yet realize it or show it, I was, as I still am, highly specialized, which is to say, narrow—a word nerd. Literature and language courses, even when they required me to pay attention and maybe concentrate a little, as in conjugating Spanish verbs, were fun for me. I walked home from school saying *hablo, hablas, habla* to myself. I joined a Boy Scout troop, in which I learned to sing "Johnny Verbeck" and the song about Three Wandering Jews, all on their way to "Amster, Amster, shh, shh, shh." That kind of shushing satisfied Scout policies and suited parents, but away from official meetings I began learning a good many unScoutlike words, especially about sex, together with information and wide-eyed speculation on the same subject, all of it ignorant and much of it wrong.

I also went camping locally a time or two, and once got a

chance to march the troop around the lawn outside the church where we met. I had learned how to do that in Miami Beach by watching the officer candidates drilling on an open lot near where I lived. But I wasn't the only Scout in that troop that knew marching orders. The other boys had absorbed enough somehow to do "By the right flank, Harch!" and "To the rear, Harch!" as I commanded and not fall over each other. Maybe those skills came untaught to boys in those war days.

My walks to and from Austin High took me past Granddad and Grandma's garage apartment. I often stopped in, especially if I thought Grandma might have made what she called a chess pie. It was not like the cloudy, too-sweet pies that restaurants call by that name. It was lustrous, glassy, sharply tiered, and light-crusted, and it tasted wonderful. Grandma, who was really my step-grandmother, wasn't otherwise a good cook, but this one dish made up for the other lacks. She and Granddad had left the farm in South Texas only a few years earlier, when he took a job with, I think, the Texas Farm Bureau. She got around in a wheelchair, as she had throughout my childhood, and she had a hearing aid the size of a slender cup and covered with soft purple cloth—the same one, I think, that she had used when I was six. She stuck the business end in her left ear and held it there while you put your mouth close to the opening and yelled. I never felt especially close to her, and though she had brought up Granddad's son and four daughters from his first marriage, she had had no idea how to treat small boys. In McGregor, when I was six and loved Omar Khayyám, she sat me down and, as I shrank away, cawed to me, in her ancient voice, "Bow-wow-wow, whose doggie art thou?" But Mother told me that it was from her that she learned to love poetry. Grandma had taught in Cuba and had what must have been perfect Spanish. A man of learning, a family friend, said she was the smartest woman he had ever met. I'm sorry I never got to know her.

Granddad's farm, forty miles northwest of Corpus Christi, caught most of the humidity of the Gulf coast and little of the sea breeze. He worked in the fields through the long, miserable summer days for half a century while his first wife and then, after her early death, the woman I called Grandma cooked, cleaned, and baby-sat in an uninsulated house. He stayed fat and, at least around us grandkids, cheerful. Mother told me much later that he could never mention his first wife, Dora Stevens, without glistening eyes and a trembling chin. She died of "childbed fever" when Mother was a year and a half old. Before her illness, she told her good friend, Givhan Fourqurean, that if she should die, she wanted her, Givhan, to be the children's mother. A few years after my real grandmother's death, "Grandma" and Granddad were married—only for the sake of child care under respectable conditions, I would bet.

I suspect that Granddad, like his daughter, "Nanty," knew romantic love only once in his life. The poor man. But we, his small grandchildren, would never have imagined that he was sad. He played with us, let us climb all over his weary body, let us feel in his pockets for candy. His voice was a genial Southern growl, and he could bark exactly like a small dog. One Christmas Eve, I lay in bed thrilled at the sound of bells running around the house, and the next morning when I stepped into the front room I saw a gleaming red tricycle under the tall Christmas tree—Santa Claus's replacement for my mashed-up kiddie-car. Granddad died in Austin in 1953, when we lived in California. Mother flew to his funeral, which was held near the old farm. She and her sisters had been very close to him.

His life became sad in another way. His son, Morris, spent so much of Granddad's money on his honeymoon in Mexico, buying extravagant gifts for his bride, that it was many years before the debts were paid off—by Granddad, with, I was told, the understanding that Morris would be removed from his father's will. Morris was a favorite uncle of mine, quiet and warm, with a twinkle and, when he did say anything, a drawl that stood out to even the rest of us drawlers. He spoke fluent Spanish, had been a good side-armed pitcher in school, and played the violin well. Later, or maybe all along, he was an alcoholic. I wonder if he was under the influence when he spent so wildly on his honeymoon. Mother and probably her other siblings blamed his bride, my Aunt Edith, for letting him do that. I wonder, though, if she altogether realized how much he was spending or whose money it was. She must later have known. The farm at Tynan was large and fertile, and yet Granddad's car was never an expensive one, and both his big wooden house and my Aunt Annis's smaller one on the same place stayed unpainted all their lives, as gray as thrown-out dishwater, rotting away in the heat and humidity. I was well grown when Mother told me that her dad had finally paid off his son's honeymoon debts.

The farm was flat and fertile, with mesquite brush all around it and the muddy Papalote Creek running through it, or, rather, lying stagnant in it. Another thing that lay in it was rattlesnakes. In Granddad's first year on the place, clearing the virgin brush, he and his helpers killed 375. There were still so many that when the girls were old enough, Granddad made a deal with them: a nickel for every dead poisonous snake. Mother and the others collected lots of nickels, especially the time she and Annis walked along opposite sides of the creek, throwing pieces of dead mesquite trunks into the water to scare up water moccasins. They got one, an uncommonly fat one, and when they had killed it, they cut it open out of curiosity. Inside were three hundred and some-odd little ones. Fifteen-plus dollars was a good bit of money in those days, but Granddad paid up. Mother was never afraid of snakes. When I was a child, we ran over a rattlesnake on the highway. It wasn't killed. I watched her saw through its neck with a pocketknife while Bob held down its head with a long stick. And Mother, you know, was a lady, a sweet and gentle woman—"the kindest person I've ever known," Nell said. Just not kind to snakes. She, by the way, felt pretty much the way we kids did about our tenting days. "I would have made a good pioneer," she said many years later.

Maybe, with Granddad, penury was a matter of allocation. The whole Montgomery clan used to spend vacations alongside the Blanco River at Wimberley, staying in a couple of large rock shelters with roofs but, in my memory, no sides unless maybe floor-to-ceiling screens, and I'm pretty sure Granddad paid the bills.

When I was about fifteen, on vacation there, Granddad announced that he had to drive to Tynan for the day to check on something at the farm.

"Can I go with you?" I said.

He was delighted. "Sho'!" he said.

Now that I have grandchildren, I can imagine how pleased he was to be asked. I learned much later, though, that he had told Mother he loved to be with small children but felt awkward with teen-agers. I know that on the drive to Tynan and back, neither of us could think of much to say. I was too old for him to bark for me, or to sing the one song I ever heard him sing. It started, "A raccoon's tail am ringed all round, / A possum's tail am bare." A slave song originally, I would guess. Mother would sing another song, a mostly sad one, that must have come down to him in the same way. It had the refrain, "Heavy load and sorry team, / Po' li'l Liza Jane. / Po' li'l Liza, so they say, / She died on the lane." A few minutes ago, on FM, I heard the late Jessye Norman sing "There is a balm in Gilead." Damn us for slavery, and I'm sure some of my ancestors were participants. Thank God, though, for the songs that came out of it. Surely they are the greatest folk music in the world.

In the spring of 1944, when I was still a junior at Austin High, Dad was sent to Peterson Field at Colorado Springs. Mother and Linda drove up to be with him, but rather than take me out of yet another school, my folks arranged for me to stay in Austin with a family we knew for the few weeks left in the school year. Then I went to join them, undoubtedly via bus. They had rented a large house at Cascade, on Ute Pass above Colorado Springs. I spent a glorious summer there, rambling in the rocky foothills and fishing in Fountain Creek.

Once, I hiked up to one of the beautiful little lakes on the Colorado Springs watershed. It was full of trout, unfished, and also, as I well knew, posted. I had just started casting when I heard a vehicle coming down the winding gravel road. I scrambled for the barbed-wire fence and skinned under it, fly rod and all. Too late. As he drove me down the road in his pickup, Mr. Dufour, the caretaker and warden, said, "I'd take you in if you weren't just a kid." The other day I read that one of the charges on the record of some figure currently in the news was "Trespassing with intent to fish." That was my crime, too, and I'm pretty sure it wasn't my last violation, though it was the last one in that location. The next time, Mr. Dufour would surely have taken me in.

At fourteen, I had become a fly-fishing snob, and I knew that the proper way to fish for trout was with a long, thin leader and a delicate fly, delicately presented. Once, though, Dad went fishing with me in the creek just across the road. While I cast a very small fly, maybe a royal coachman, and watched it float elegantly down the current on the tips of its tail and hackles, barely getting wet, he jammed salmon eggs, a worm, and maybe a grasshopper onto a large hook and with a heavy sinker on the line slammed it all with a splash into the current just below the bridge. He immediately caught a thirteen-inch rainbow trout. I caught nothing.

If Dad didn't know how to sell himself to prospective employers, he knew how to sell himself to fish. When I was seven or eight and we were on vacation at Eagle Nest Lake in northern New Mexico, he cut an aspen sapling (not illegal back then), trimmed it, wrapped a guide onto the tip end, used cord also to attach his practically antique, single-action, open-faced casting reel onto the butt, and with a heavy sinker cast a baited hook far out into the lake. Two fly fishermen close to him, visibly scornful, cast and cast without luck. Dad caught two large, beautiful trout—I remember seeing one jump high above the surface as it fought.

And again, thirty years later, when we were vacationing in Ontario, Dad and I went out in separate rowboats at night to fish for walleyed pike on opposite sides of a small lake. Other fishermen were all around. Now and then, one would say something to a companion in a quiet voice that the water amplified. I could hear their oars knocking against their boats. I cast for quite a while, without result. "Don," Dad's voice came resonantly across the water, "I've caught two nice walleyes and a two-pound smallmouth bass. Come over here." I was as embarrassed as if he had announced to the whole lake that his hemorrhoids were acting up, but I went, and cast, and of course caught nothing.

We moved out of Cascade and down to the city in time for my senior year in what was then Colorado Springs High School. Our house, a roomy, white-frame one, was on a short and beautiful street, Tyler Place, off North Cascade Avenue. When we looked west along the street, we could see Pikes Peak. Until it got too cold, I slept on a glassed-in porch on the second floor, up among the maple leaves. It was on balance a wonderful year for me in school—my fifth high school. True, I barely squeezed through solid geometry, trigonometry, and physics, and that was only because my math teacher, no doubt having seen my scores on whatever SAT equivalents I had taken, must have felt somehow at fault for my performance. She shook her head as she marked down my E—the grade that meant I had flunked but they wanted to let me graduate. "You have a *good* mind," she told me. I didn't, though, not at math, and I had even less of the discipline I needed to get a real passing grade in it.

That was one unwonderful part of my senior year. Another was girls. Still fourteen for part of the year, awkward and naïve, I wanted desperately to touch one of those delightful bodies—Patty King's, for instance, in my history class. When she happened to look my way, I showed my thoughts by blushing furiously—I could feel the blood sizzling over my face. That happened at least twice. Some days after one of those incidents, when I was in an English class that had just let out for the day, another girl, Virginia Hatch, turned squarely around from her seat at the front and stared at me meaningfully with her beautiful, slightly slanted eyes. I performed as expected. I'm sure Patty had told her what I would do. I was socially helpless. "I'm a woman-hater," I started telling people. I was like hell.

Otherwise, what a year it was. I went out for cross-country running in the fall and for track in the spring, not making the team but not disgracing myself either. With a friend a couple of years older than I, and whatever other guys we could round up, I played touch football on a sloping lot above the creek, which was the only open grassy space we could find. In those days, the cross-body block was still legal, and I found that by using it, leaving my feet, I could bring down boys a lot bigger and older than I. Dad got in a game with us once and lined up opposite me. I threw a block into him and knocked him over. Wow. But he wasn't going to get careless again. A few plays later, when I tried the block that had worked before, nothing was there but air. He was close to fifty then but the quickest, most elusive defender I ever faced in my many sandlot games.

I had loved football since the days of Sammy Baugh and Davey O'Brien, but it never occurred to me to try out for the Terrors team. Though I wasn't quite as slow, awkward, and small as in my pre-teen years, my image of myself hadn't caught up with my bodily development. A significant event in school narrowed that gap a great deal. One day in P.E. we were given big, heavily padded boxing gloves and told to pair off. My opponent was Frank Robinson, nineteen years old, burly though overweight, who for some reason had been discharged by the Marine Corps.

We agreed just to spar, but right away he drove me into the bleachers with a furious attack. I got up, surprised, and flailed back at him. Neither of us knew anything about boxing except just to score as many hard punches as possible. I was hit in the face over and over, with small electric jolts, and I knew I was landing some blows of my own. After a minute or so I saw out of the corner of my eye that all the other boxers had stopped their matches to watch us. I remembered something Dad had told me, and I lunged forward with a straight left that flattened Frank's face. "Wah!" the audience yelled. We finally stopped or were stopped. The next day, after English class, a sturdy classmate named Ed Colt came up to me.

"That was quite a show you and Robinson put on yesterday," he said.

"Yeah," I said, "that guy hits pretty hard."

"Oh, you was beating the shit out of him."

I had had no idea. Those words went a long way toward dissolving my image of myself as a picked-on kid. I wish I could thank Ed Colt. He would be, probably, ninety-five now. Maybe he is. If there had been no coronavirus and if my senior class at what is now Palmer High School had held a reunion in 2020, it would have been the seventy-fifth. Would I have been the only participant, a reuniter with myself? I think I know one thing: if Patty King or Virginia Hatch had been there, too, and had stared at me, I wouldn't have blushed.

IV.

I was sick of being a kid among young adults, and I decided to work for a year before I started college. When Dad came home from the war and started a job as a rewriteman for *The Denver Post*, I got on as a copy boy. That was the day of manual typewriters and real paper. My job was to pull stories off the spike on the news editor's desk and run them up the steep metal stairs to the composing room. I ran lots of up-and-down miles, blithely, in that year. Oh, to have such knees again, and such lungs. Once, when the nightside copy boy was sick, I ran the stairs for sixteen hours, a double shift. No problem, though I doubt that I got paid time-and-a-half.

The newsroom was an exciting place to me. I had just read Gene Fowler's *Timber Line*, a salty biography of *The Denver Post*. I looked around and, wow, saw people who were actually in a book. It was a big room. Dad worked quite a way across it. I barely have an image of him at his desk. My workstation, which meant my chair, was handy to the open part of the U-shaped copy desk, where stories turned in by reporters were read, fitted out with headlines, and assigned their place and shape in the paper. The copy desk head, a small, red-haired man named Heber Smith, sat in the slot and was the last set of newsroom eyes to see every story. He would spike a piece of copy and half-turn my way, muttering something unintelligible and, I was pretty sure, dire. Once in a while, he would turn all the way toward me and call "hot stuff." I would jump for it and run upstairs. I chafed at his usual words, though, and finally one day I confronted him.

"What did you say?" I demanded with back-alley belligerency.

"I said there's no hurry on this," he said, mildly. If I had had a less defensive view of the adult world months before that exchange, I could have saved myself a good many trips up and down the stairs.

One of the reporters, Joy Swift, a slender, pretty woman, white-haired but probably no older than sixty, talked with me in a motherly way about skiing, which she loved. That Christmas, my folks gave me a pair of very long, very used skis. I rode the bus to Berthoud Pass, where there was a rope tow. I had read a little about doing snowplows and stem christies, and at the top of the tow I swung around, somehow not crossing my skis, and plunged downslope. I have an image of myself as if I were an onlooker. I am ludicrously out of control, with one ski on the snow and the other waving in the air. I fall. I get up, try to scrape snow into my sitzmark with an edge, then hurtle onward and fall again. This time, one ski comes off. Fortunately, I'm close to the bottom and manage to get out of other skiers' way.

At home, I discover that the bindings on both skis are worn out and won't keep a grip on my boot soles. So I couldn't have controlled the skis even if I had known how. Trying to fix them, I fill the gaps with lead slugs from the composing room at the *Post*. (I hope I asked permission.) That works long enough that the next time I ski I complete one teetering turn before the slugs pop out. Not an auspicious start at a sport that ought to be as graceful as ballet and as exciting as sky dives. Somehow I got through that winter and learned to manage at least beginners' slopes. I was hooked.

Before my interim year was up, Dad had yet another job offer: move to California and ghost-write the newspaper column of

Upton Close, who wanted to devote more time to his work as a radio commentator. Dad and Close were compatible politically, with opinions that now would relegate their work to right-wing-fringe publications. Dad grew up on a farm and then in a small West Texas city, among second-generation settlers, all of them white and with names as British Isles in origin as Williams is. To him, they were, if not quite the only real Americans, at least the realest ones. He was convinced that people with other backgrounds and with left-wing opinions hoped to destroy freedom and independence in the United States, and he observed that many Jews were on the left politically. If they were not outright communist conspirators, he believed, they were fellow travelers or deluded parlor pinks. Like Senator Joseph McCarthy, he shot scatterbore.

But there were at that time real communists at work in our government, with sympathizers in the press. Anyone who called attention to them, including Dad and Upton Close, had better duck, because retaliation was savage. Attacked, Dad fought back in his own newsletter, the *Williams Intelligence Summary*. His conviction that he was saving Western civilization and being attacked by its despoilers became an obsession—his sole topic of conversation. He grew hard for Mother and the rest of us to bear. His marriage was in danger, and he didn't understand why.

"When a woman gets to be forty-five, all she wants you to do is let her alone," he told me.

Once, when I was home from college, he let us know that he had to go to Los Angeles on a top-secret mission—he couldn't tell us what. Years later, he told me about visiting a prostitute in Los Angeles, "a nice young girl," and said that was "the last time I had to do that." I'm sure she was the secret mission. Somehow, my folks stayed together, and Dad eventually gave up his obsession with politics. That was about the time he sold the little company that was beginning to market his addressing machine. I think money and the pleasant challenges of genteel ranching took over from his determination to save the world. I know that his marriage was happy again.

Bob, my big brother—he is actually a few inches shorter than I, though huskier—spent most of his Army career playing the piano for the troops. He had tried to be, among other things, a navigator, but his Williams absentmindedness washed him out: he kept forgetting to do the easy chore of calculating and reporting the plane's position every ten minutes. He never went overseas. After the war, he used the G.I. Bill of Rights to enroll in the Lamont School of Music at Denver University. Starting as a child, he had taken piano lessons from our mother, and by his late teens he had a good technique and was clearly meant for a musical career.

He found a place to live in Denver: the attic of an orthodox Jewish mortuary, Feldman's, on York Street cattycornered from City Park. In return for the free lodging, he would answer the phone at night. *We* would answer it, or one of us would—I joined him there in August 1946, when I also had enrolled at DU. Calls at night weren't frequent, but when one came in, we could earn a dollar if we wanted to go along and help load and unload. We usually did. A dollar meant something, and we were always considerately given the foot-end to carry.

Dad, having heard me sing around the house, urged me to take voice lessons. I signed up for private ones with a teacher at Lamont, though my major was German, not music. I needed the language because by then I wanted to sing Schubert and Schumann like my artistic ideal, the great Danish tenor Aksel Schiøtz. For both the language and the singing, my teachers in Denver were marvelous. Their influence has guided me ever since. Frau Fanny Keller, a Viennese fugitive from Hitler, spoke a cultured German, complete with the tongue-trilled *r* that singers use instead of the back-in-the-throat gurgle of most Germans' speech. She conversed in German with her students from

the very first day. Eleanor Leffingwell, long divorced or wid-
owed—I'm not sure which—taught me the freedom of produc-
tion that is the one great requisite of good singing. Both women,
though I didn't realize it at the time, were also mother figures to
me, and at sixteen, far from home, I needed mothering.

I needed fathering, too, and Bob, bless him, provided that,
along with wise and gentle big-brothering. He showed me how
to warm corn tortillas for tacos, wrapping them first in a damp
dish towel. He told me, "Don, you sure do a half-assed job of
shaving," which was right; I reformed. When we went winter
camping in the mountains, he cut the poles for a lean-to and
thatched them with fir boughs, legal activities in those days,
while I tried to help by doing some elementary chore like fill-
ing our canteens from the sparkling little stream close at hand.
Though he was a long way from handy with girls and of course
had no car, he did date. He told me about the cute girl from
Kentucky who had him to her house for dinner. Before that was
served, he told me, her mother said, "Bahh-bee, don'ch want
t'go t'th' bayth-room?" He liked the girl but couldn't stand the
mother, and that was the end of a promising romance.

In the basement of the mortuary was our family's great old
Steinway; Mother must have given it to Bob, and I can imag-
ine how sad she was to be without it. Bob spent many an hour
practicing the Schumann *Carnaval* and the Beethoven *Waldstein*
sonata on it, and he accompanied me when I practiced "Star vici-
no" or "Verdi prati." But enough of music. On the way to or from
the basement one night Bob made a discovery. Through a small
window by the staircase he caught sight of a lighted upstairs
room in a house across the way. A young woman was taking off
her nursing costume. The next night, Bob called me urgently to
come and look. He handed me the field glasses, hurrying.

There she stood with her back to the window, naked. Lord,
what a sight. Except for my mother, I had never before seen a

woman without clothes on. Neither had Bob, I'm sure. It was an astounding experience, delicious and thrilling. It was the confirmation of all my speculations of, by then, several longing years. And it was typical of Bob to let me use the field glasses for a few seconds, depriving himself. Oh, I gave them back to him before it was too late.

We couldn't both leave the mortuary at night. When we went camping together, we imposed on our friend the mortician, a middle-aged, red-faced, Irish American Catholic. He stayed for us a good many Saturday nights, bless him. I'm afraid Bob and I never thanked him enough for sacrificing that time with his family. It didn't occur to us to give him a present, not that we could have afforded much of one. His name was Sweeney, though the elderly, Yiddish-speaking Jews who made the mortuary a gathering place called him Sheeney instead: "I wouldn't call my friend a pig."

Sweeney would come upstairs to listen with me to my seventy-eight-rpm acoustic records of John McCormack, the great Irish tenor, played on my cheap, single-shot turntable. (I got those records for twenty-five cents each out of the tall stacks at the Salvation Army store on Larimer Street. I still have them.) He told Bob and me about the "come-all-ye" musical gatherings he used to join in the Irish part of, I think, Philadelphia. He loved music; had heard the famous contralto, Ernestine Schumann-Heink. I suppose Sweeney's gruesome job was routine to him, but I felt sorry for him. I hope he had a long and happy life.

I took a bus down York to my classes at DU and also to my voice lessons at Lamont. We had a Schwinn bicycle, single-speed and fat-tired, of course, but I don't remember ever riding it to school. What we mostly used it for was to go to Hummel's delicatessen or to a Chinese restaurant across the street from the state capitol and bring back a paper carton of rich beef stew from the one place or chow mein from the other. Often, we made tacos from ground beef, cooked on our single-burner hot plate, with cut-up fresh tomatoes and onions and corn tortillas—no salsa of any kind, just tabasco sauce, which we used liberally. No beer, of course, though I can hardly imagine tacos, these days, without it. I had never touched any alcoholic drink, even the few times when Dad had wine with his meal and offered me a sip. In some ways, I was a prude.

Food of our kind was cheap. It had to be; I don't know what Bob did for money, but Dad sent me $42.50 every two weeks, or maybe every ten days. Once, he sent each of us a gift of five dollars. Bob saved his for dates or camping gear, but I, a budding hedonist, gave myself a steak dinner at Pell's restaurant on East Colfax. I hope I tipped more than a quarter

Everybody called my voice teacher Leff, though I put a "Miz" before it. She was tall, middle-aged, and angular like a Valkyrie, and like all great teachers she practically embedded her own intensity in the wills of her students. It was imperative that you concentrated, that you practiced, that you opened your mouth the way she said. I got by for a whole year resisting the last of those imperatives for fear that the resonance, if any, would escape if I opened too wide. I also resisted the total release necessary to let my soft palate plaster itself against the inside-back of my nose, because when that happened, I felt a frightening buzz in my nasal passages. I was afraid of sounding like one of the singers with the Light Crust Doughboys, the country-music group founded by W. Lee (Pappy) O'Daniel, who won the governorship of Texas largely because of his connection with them.

Leff was patient with me; she thought she heard promise in my unresonant kid voice, though when I heard it on a record I made in those days I wasn't impressed. Finally, in November of my second school year with her, I gave in and quit gripping with my throat. It was an act of abandon, like stepping out of an in-flight airplane, but the tone leaped into a forward-driving vibrancy, and when I heard myself on a new record I was amazed and proud. Singers do hear themselves, but not accurately, not as if they were on the other side of the room. This sound was steady, warm, and more nearly grown-up than before. Leff had perfect pitch and also a perfect ear for what a voice was doing and not doing. "I can hear the grass grow," she would say, with justification. She told me I could be making big money as a singer in two years.

Another student of Miz Leff's was a cute soprano named Winnie Linsenmaier. She was about my age, not a college student yet, and she sang with lightness and clarity. She and I did the Masetto-Zerlina duet from Mozart's *Don Giovanni* (I was still a baritone). I was smitten. I actually dared to ask her to double-date with me, the other couple being another Leffingwell student named Sam Chean and his girlfriend. Sam drove his car. I think we all went to a movie, and when Sam stopped at Winnie's house afterward, I sat still and said to her, "Well, good night." Sam made an expostulating sound, but Winnie, though flustered, said good night back to me, let herself out her side of the car, and walked to her door alone. I knew instantly that I had done an unspeakable thing, but there was nothing I could do, only feel humiliated for days afterward. Winnie for some reason agreed to another date a few weeks later, and this time I got out of the car, opened her door, and walked with her to her front door, not even conceiving that I might ask for a kiss. In such wise did I waste my youth.

Seventy-three years after my Denver University days, I am still aggrieved at one of my professors. His name was Woellhaf, if I spell it right, and his subject was English, though it was called Basic Communications. He gave me C's for all three quarters, the only times I ever made less than A in English anywhere. I'm pretty sure I know why. It wasn't just that I wrote kiddish stuff, silly and sentimental. That might have got me B's rather than

A's, and justly so. But I was comparatively an old hand at sifting letters into words and eyedropping words into sentences. Surely my spelling and grammar were worth better than C's.

It happened, though, that it was Woellhaf who had interviewed me at registration. He had obviously looked into my background.

"Would you say that your father is a fascist?" he asked me.

If I had been older—say, ninety—I would have answered, "A fascist believes in ruthless tyranny, in concentration camps or death by torture for all who disagree. My father was born loving freedom. Of course he is not a fascist. Are you a communist?" I was sixteen. I said, "No."

Woellhaf, actually, taught me some worthwhile things. He read eloquently from *Hamlet*, and he introduced me and the rest of the class to Thurber's "The Secret Life of Walter Mitty," which alone, if I had written it, would still seem to me to have constituted a worthwhile life's work. The Woellhaf classes weren't wasted on me. But I'm sure it was my parentage that got me those C's.

When you live in Denver, as in most of Colorado, your days are informed by mountains. You watch their tones and shadows as a sharer, as part of the same picture. If you are young and energetic, and especially if your big brother is Bob, you get into that part of the picture as often as possible, wearing boots and carrying a pack. Bob taught me how to keep drawing an Army-surplus mummy sleeping bag toward me as I rolled it up, squeezing air out of the down so that what I lashed onto my pack board wouldn't take much more space than the nylon tarp or the wool sweater. He showed me how to sharpen my sheath knife, first with an oiled whet rock and then with the back side of my broad leather belt, until the blade would shave hair off my legs. (I get my kitchen knives—leftovers from Nell's cooking days—sharp enough to dice onions nicely or to cut a top sirloin into stew-sized cubes, but when I try them on my arms, the hairs spring right back. I've lost the knack, or maybe the patience.) In the foothills, day hiking, Bob showed me warblers I would never have seen otherwise, and currant bushes to harvest by the handful. On the alpine tundra, he introduced me to whortleberries, half the diameter of English peas but astoundingly flavorful, surely the best berries in the world.

On one warm-season hike, I was able to contribute something comparable. We had stopped at a little lake high up in foothills, and I caught three or four Eastern brook trout that were not much bigger than pet goldfish. I cleaned them and put them whole in the hot ashes of our fire. We held them in our hands as we ate them. It hadn't been more than a half-hour since they were swimming in water that was perfectly clear and timberline cold. A restaurant that could serve fish as full of flavor as that would get a Milky Way's-worth of Michelin stars. I was proud to have contributed something worthwhile; Bob never cared much for fishing. He taught me mountains, though, and heightened my love of them. I got a book out of them much later, and years and years of pleasure that were stalled by COVID but have returned to the extent of walks on easy trails in the Sangre de Cristo range of New Mexico, a six-hour drive from my house.

In May of 1948 I had finished two years of college and still hated being younger than everybody else. I took advantage of an arrangement whereby eighteen-year-olds could fulfill their military obligations by doing one year of active service, limited to the United States, and then five years in the Reserve. I volunteered. It wasn't cowardice; I just wanted to get that part of my life done with and move on, though I knew not what to. Nearly all my year was at Camp (now Fort) Hood, in central Texas. It was a year of semi-torpor, spent amid chiggers, Clorox-tasting water, and nightly sessions of anatomically detailed conquest-boasting by a group of teen-aged voluptuaries at the far end of the barracks.

True, there was some diversion even in those tales: the accents. A kid from the Bronx kept saying, "Hey, youse guys, knock if ohff." One from Georgia would say, starting in a drawn-out falsetto, "WHO-oo are YEW tawkin' to?" But I heard nothing original, imaginative, or truly funny, nothing like the erudite nightly barracks conversation that impressed and intimidated Dad in 1918. He, of course, was among future officers, not teen-agers whose only common impulse was not to be soldiers longer than necessary. One night in my barracks, one of the voices speculated that I might have things to tell, too. "A quiet mouse gets his cheese," he said. I didn't reply; I was ashamed of my innocence. My thoughts, Lord knows, were not innocent. When my shapely distant cousin, Margaret—not the one who became a rector and lived nearly to a hundred—wore tight shorts, as she often did, it took all my will to keep from touching her where they clung.

Among the other silent and probably inexperienced soldiers around me in the barracks were some wonderfully generous guys. One named Weir, from Socorro, New Mexico, noticed in the chow hall that I cleaned up all the beans or hash in my mess kit and still looked hungry. He started overfilling his own kit and pouring some of the excess into mine. He said he told himself, "Well, Williams requires more food than I do." I did. I have been blessed with a metabolism like Dagwood's. But what a swell guy Weir was. And there was Cantrell, from I think North Carolina, whose Military Occupational Specialty was delivering the mail every day. As the center fielder on our company softball team he saw me, in left field, misjudge a fly ball and run back, cursing, to grab it off the ground. "That's all right, that's all right," he called, and afterward he took pains to tell me he could never have thrown from deep left field to third base as I had done. I hope both of those guys had happy and fulfilling civilian lives. Maybe they're still around; I haven't been granted exclusive possession of the nineties.

After basic training, I became the company information NCO, though I wasn't yet a noncommissioned officer. My two years of college were a factor, I'm sure. My duties were to sit in the dayroom every weekday, in season listening to Gordon McLendon, "The Old Scotchman," give vivid play-by-play accounts of baseball games he knew only from ticker-tape reports. "The bases are f.o.b., full of Brooklyns," he would say. The batter might be "turkey-neck Ewell Blackwell." I don't think I suspected that McLendon wasn't actually in the park, watching.

Those were great baseball days. I "heard" Bob Feller and Warren Spahn pitch, and Stan Musial and Ralph Kiner bat. Once a week I performed a duty other than baseball listening. I read a canned report on current events to the gathered troops. And one day I did what soldiers are noted for: I helped paint a barracks. My Army life was dull, my adventures few. I did make a friend, Donn Taylor, with whom I still correspond occasionally and who, a retired Army major, is one day older than I. We and another friend often went to the Post Exchange in the evenings, bought large cartons of hard, dry stuff that passed for ice cream, and poured hot black coffee over it so it would be soft enough to get a spoon into. Probably because of that routine, I put on more weight than ever before or after. When I went home on furlough, Dad shook his head and said, "Don's going to have a belly like John McCormack."

In basic training, I hadn't minded the marches, being used to hiking, and I enjoyed the day of target shooting when, using the sight-picture-refining and trigger-squeezing skills I had learned from Bob and practiced on his single-shot .22, I made easily the highest scores in the company on both the M-1 rifle and the little carbine. In the spring, when my company organized a softball team, I tried out for it, though I hadn't played an inning since the fourth grade, and in fact all through my childhood and early teens had been ashamed of the way I threw—

"like a goddamn girl," a classmate said. Dad had tried to teach me to get my body into the motion, something he had always done without being taught. I was afraid to do that, as if it would amount, somehow, to a leap into space. He gave up on me when I resisted, just as, later, I resisted Miz Leff's instructions to quit hanging on to my voice. Abandon frightened me.

So I was surprised when I made the team, especially since I made it largely because of something I had never suspected I owned: my throwing arm. I don't know how or when I had finally learned to use it right. Otherwise, though, I was a long way from stardom. I let that fly ball land twenty feet behind me. I got only one hit in our two or three games, and then, on base, I fell for the first baseman's trick of faking a throw back to the pitcher and then tagging me out. But the success at throwing, like the boxing match with Frank Robinson, did a lot to improve my self-image. To that extent, the Army had, as the saying goes, made a man out of me.

In September 1949, when I had done my year of heroic service to my country and was a civilian again and had just spent a central Texas summer in an uninsulated barracks, I headed to Colorado to cool off. I found a room in a Denver boarding house and worked for a few months at The Record Shop, where the owner, Henry Yohannan, played Bach records for himself and his employees when no customers were present. Then, at my folks' urging, I took the bus home to Santa Ana, California, and enrolled in Whittier College, a decent small school of Quaker influence. There, I had a poetry class under Charles W. Cooper, who, though I didn't realize it at the time, was as important an influence on my later turns and meanderings as Miz Leff and Fanny Keller had been. He taught us imagery and metaphor, iamb and trochee, and even a kind of foot I have rarely seen on a page. His imitative formula for that one was: "And lastly remember, the amphibrach's rocking, dear pupil." And he taught the interplay of sound and sense, which is to say, poetry. I wish I had realized at the time how important those lessons would remain to me, so I could have thanked Dr. Cooper. I do still have his book, *Preface to Poetry.*

College, in most ways, bored me as much as the Army had. I finished the semester and took out for Colorado Springs. I found a room, or half a room—my roommate was an uneducated, hard-drinking fellow of about my age—in what had been a garage and took meals next door in a very large, rundown, fish-scaled boarding house on North Cascade Avenue. Dinner, with a dozen of us around the table under a threatening chandelier in the high-ceilinged dining room, ran heavily to mashed potatoes and butter beans. We got meat, too, but I think just one serving apiece. The owner and cook, a large, elderly woman with a hip problem, hobbled back and forth, bringing more stacks of pasty white bread and refilling ice-tea glasses. One boarder, an upper-middle-aged man who sold the brand of shoes you could get only from salesmen unattached to a store, had the infuriating habit of chewing with his mouth open. I tried to eat before or after him

Another of the tenants was a woman in her late forties who had a whiny Slavic accent and a radio. By virtue of seniority—she had lived there forever—she had a choice second-floor room with a balcony. She invited me in on Saturday afternoons to listen to the Metropolitan Opera with her. I think we raised a few eyebrows, since the rules said no men could be in the women's rooms. I considered her age too great to activate the rule. I was interested only in her radio.

Job-hunting, I tried the Peerless Printing Co., on Colorado Avenue in Old Town. Robert Erickson, who with his brother, Melvin, owned the business, told me they needed an editor for the little weekly paper they put out, the *Colorado Springs Independent.* The previous editor had quit when Robert sat her down and showed her all the typos in that week's paper.

The job was mine. I rode the bus to and from it daily, and I did such news as I had any notion how to find. I also sold ads, cut and pasted the circulation list, and stood by the printer, reading Page One upside down in metal type, while we decided which story went where. I wrote a silly column that was called, at Mother's suggestion, "Rocky Mountain Rambles" but wasn't often about hiking or the mountains. A few feet away from my desk, Robert, and a few feet farther along, Melvin, typed all day on the big Linotype machines, drudging ceaselessly, ruining their backs. My job should have taught me something about newsgathering or should have led me to read up on the subject. I learned nothing, read nothing. I thought a meeting of the Rotary Club was news.

I coasted for seven months before the Williams restlessness set in and I left. For a while, I worked as a sporting goods clerk at, I think, the Montgomery Ward's store in Colorado Springs. (It may have been Sears, Roebuck instead.) The department manager there was impressed when he saw me rolling up a sleeping bag, keeping the roll taut the way Bob had taught me. I don't know how long I was there or why I left, though probably for the usual reason: boredom. I worked as a carpenter's helper for a while. I remember prancing along, full of exuberant energy, on a crisp morning with a floor joist on my shoulder, and the carpenter, a man in his sixties, shaking his head and smiling in wonder. Once in a while, youth is all it's supposed to be.

Since I was, as always, taking voice lessons and had no place to vocalize, I sometimes sneaked into a practice room at Colorado College. Once when I was there, I heard someone playing Beethoven nicely on the piano and waited at the door to see who would come out. It was an attractive woman, Ellie Wagner— six years older than I, it turned out, and far more sophisticated, a widow already and soon to head for Chicago to be married again. She indulged me by having coffee with me several times.

We talked poetry, and I tried to indoctrinate her with Dad's extremist politics, to which at the time I unquestioningly subscribed. She heard me out, not commenting but surely horrified. You couldn't reasonably say she and I were dating, but I regretted her age and unavailability. She was wise, talented, and kind. I dated two or three girls during my months in Colorado Springs and then, at my folks' urging, went home again. It was the summer of 1951. I was not quite twenty-two. I still didn't have a car.

V.

My folks must have wanted to make up for the parenting I had missed in my six years of being on my own and mostly alone. If that was their wish, I took full advantage of it. I lived at home for three years while I drove my first car, a ceaselessly troublesome 1939 Studebaker, to my jobs, first as circulation manager of *The Anaheim Bulletin* before Disneyland and then as a classified ad salesman for *The Fullerton News-Tribune*. When I found a job by mail as a reporter for *The Spokesman-Review* in Spokane, Washington, and headed back into solitude for a while, surely they were relieved. I had lived with them for three years, a grown man, eating Mother's delicious cooking, contributing no money and very little work to the household, spending most of my time at work or on dates or in the mountains hiking with Bob, who also lived in Santa Ana, or skiing. They wouldn't be lonely with Bob there and with my sister, Linda, at home, in her mid-teens and clearly on her way to a career as a violinist. They played Scrabble with the next-door neighbors. Dad's younger brother, Carl, lived in Long Beach and sometimes visited for a few hours, not always drunk.

My move, that time, finally marked the end of my childhood. Before, when I was away from home, I had sampled from a tray of uninspiring jobs. Now I had an entree. Newspaper reporting and, later, editing were exactly right for me, and I think I knew it from the start. It was still a good time to go into that field. Newspapers had barely begun to suffer from the competition of television. They had plenty of news jobs for such as I, and the salaries, Lord knows, can't have cost them much except on the big papers. I imagine that I, as a cub in Spokane, made less than sixty-five dollars a week. I lived in a boarding house, as usual, and by then was driving a senile Plymouth. The paper put me on the night police beat, of course, and not more than a couple of weeks after I started, there came a call on the police radio: a gunfight outside a supermarket. When I got there, a man was lying on his back on the parking lot with his face shot away, and another was sitting close to him, handcuffed and with an expression that a newcomer to hell must wear, shocked, hopeless, and, beyond those, as I have since supposed, high on some powerful drug.

One of the two deputies there, a chubby, boyish fellow in his twenties, was standing next to a car with its back door open, reporting to a note-taking superior, probably the sheriff. In the unrestricted ways of that era, I was able to stand next to them and make my own notes. The deputies had been tipped off to a planned robbery, the young one said, and apparently given a description of the robbers' car. The young deputy had gone up to it, peered into the back seat, and jumped back. "Jesus Christ!" he said, "they're in there, and they've got guns." The shooting started, but neither officer was hurt. I talked briefly to a kid in his late teens who was sitting nearby in a Model A Ford coupe. He had been there all through the gunfight, he said, but no, he hadn't really seen it.

"Were you lying down?" I asked, pointing to the floor of his car.

"You ain't just a-whistling I was," he said.

That was a big story for a raw cub, and I succeeded in messing it up, at least at the start. Somewhere I had read that it was good to get a person's name into the lead sentence. So my story began with the information that John Q. Somebody, 31, was shot to death and Pete X. Somebody Else, 27, was captured in a gun battle with sheriff's deputies on the Whatsit supermarket lot last night. How the copy desk could let the story go that way, I've never figured out. At least the body of the story went much better, and of course it got the banner on Page 1. No byline, though. In those days, *The Spokesman-Review* put those only on staff-written stories from other towns—to show that the paper had really sent somebody out of town, I suppose.

I stayed in Spokane three months and then was sent to Moses Lake, Washington, on plains drier than West Texas, to cover that town and four others in the new Columbia Basin Project. I lived in a dingy little two-room house with a jittering teletype next to the bed, reporting mostly irrigation news and small courthouse stories but also the case of a glamorous young red-haired woman who was accused of killing her baby. That case was finally dropped for lack of evidence. Socially, the main and almost only activity in my ten-months' stay was skiing. I went in with four or five other young people, all of them married or engaged, to lease a cabin on Stevens Pass for the winter, and the deep snows of the Cascades provided us some delightful weekends.

Those weren't enough, not at that stage of my life. Most of the settlers on the irrigation project were veterans, with young wives and small children, if any. Young single women scarcely existed in Moses Lake, as far as I could determine. I had only two dates while I was there, each with a different girl. So I moved again, this time to Amarillo, Texas, where I imagined there would be beautiful girls. There were.

The *Amarillo Globe-News* had both a morning-and-Sunday and an afternoon paper, both of them flourishing in 1956, when the city had a population of not much more than one hundred thousand. The combined circulation of the papers was at least eighty-eight thousand. Those are grim facts to me, because today, in a city with about two hundred thousand residents, the pitiful remnant of the *Globe-News* has no more than eight thousand subscribers to the printed product. Nobody could love the paper now, doddering, weak-minded wreck that it is, but I love the memory of it as it was when it and I were in our primes. And when two other employees, named Nell and Jane, were also in theirs. I loved both girls, at the same time and in very different ways. Largely because of one of them, I have loved Amarillo and the Texas Panhandle for sixty-four years and will do so until I die. Thanks, *Globe-News* that was, for her that was.

I covered police and sheriff's news, sometimes courts, sometimes feature stories and always whatever came across the city editor's desk when I was in the office and free. The city editor was Paul Timmons, a man of silent competence. He told me almost nothing, but he taught me by editing my copy. Once, when he had glanced at a story of mine, he called me over and handed it back. "Put the lead on top," he said. That was all, but how good it was to be instructed even a little. How good to work in a newsroom again, to have a chair in that clattering orchestra whose director used a thick-leaded Eagle pencil for a baton and seldom looked up at the players. Professionally, I spent an uneventful ten months on the *Globe-News*. If I wrote a single major story, I can't remember it.

Unprofessionally, though, the months in Amarillo were the most eventful ones of my life. Jane (I withhold her surname because she is still alive), who did some reporting and also some work as an assistant to this or that executive, caught my eye right away, partly because of her pretty face and sweet smile and partly because she dressed as simply in the newsroom as a little girl playing dolls with a friend. We started dating very quickly, and I was soon smitten. Jane had indeed the trustingness, the sweet wonder, the playful innocence, of a child. She made me feel protective at the same time I, too, became ten years old. I was Tom Sawyer; she was Becky Thatcher. We loved each other desperately. So what held me back? Why didn't we get engaged and marry and spend our lives in endlessly fresh love? That was it, I think. I knew that I was a child, knew that living from then on with a woman so sweet and young would perpetuate my immaturity. Was I remembering the Depression, when my dad and my mother and my granddad seemed almost proud of working so hard and having so little? They were the kind of real grownups I wanted to be and needed help to be. Help was there, thank God.

The other fellow employee who had caught my eye was Nell Osborne. She dressed like a lady of quiet taste, including high heels, and she stood notably straight. When she walked through the newsroom, male heads turned. One of the copy editors asked her something once, shortly after I started work there. When she had answered, he turned to Charles Whippo, the news editor, who was quite deaf, and said loudly, "Twenty-three." That was her waist measurement. The question, in those days, had been meant, and was taken, as a compliment. I doubt that, even at my harmless age, I could get by with asking it today.

Nell and I smiled and nodded at each other from the first, and after a few days she would lay a hand softly on my shoulder for a second as she walked past my desk. On our first date, we went to the Embers steakhouse, unpretentious and dinerlike. She had an unpretentious steak, something like a top sirloin, medium rare, and the first of several thousand Cokes I would see her drink in the next five decades and more. To my surprise, I got a kiss at her door that night, and it was so very warm and sweet, so womanly, that as I walked back to my car I told myself, "I'm going to marry Nell Osborne." By then, though, I had had several dates with Jane. I don't know why, but after a few weeks I told Nell how those had affected me.

"I guess I'm in love with her," I said.

"I guess you are," Nell said, with sadness and her unfailing dignity. Forty, fifty years later, she told me that in those days, "I used to cry myself to sleep." She did so that night, I would bet. It's good that young love afflicts only the young. The old couldn't survive it. At that point in my youth, I was staggering under the charms of the delightful Jane. She warmed and enfeebled me like Rodgers and Hammerstein, like Cole Porter. I had begun to realize, though, that that music might cool after enough repetitions. More and more, I heard the eternal strains, close at hand, of Mozart, of Schumann, and Fauré. Those had also a hint of Baptist Sunday school in them, and of turning windmills. Nell grew up on a wheat farm and cattle ranch northeast of Amarillo, near the town of Panhandle. Between the ages of ten and fifteen, she killed at least two of the family's chickens every day, cleaned them, dipped them in boiling water, plucked them, and delivered them to her mother to fry for the men when they came in from the fields at noon. I figure, conservatively, that she pulled the heads off 1,250 chickens before she started Panhandle High School. She rode the bus there until she graduated, as valedictorian, and went off to North Texas State College (now the University of North Texas), at Denton, a little north of Dallas.

When I met her, in August 1955, she had received a journalism degree three months before. She wasn't a reporter at the *Globe-News*, though, except for a little of what was called women's news—houses, cooking, parties, clothes. Her main job was as secretary to Louise Evans, a demanding, mini-cigar-smoking, rather brilliant woman whose position at the paper may not have had a name but which, in her hands, became a power in bringing about the large medical center in Amarillo, including a pretty little dammed-up pond that people soon called Lake Louise. She and Nell got along well—hit it off, in fact. I wonder if that was true of any other of her secretaries, before or after. Nell had a great capacity, always, for dealing with odd employers, and, if they were intelligent and original, enjoying them. She understood what they wanted and knew how to improve on it without their catching on. She was smarter than they. Some of them were smart enough to know that, and all, I think, were smart enough to love and appreciate her.

I took longer falling in love with Nell than I had with Jane. I recognized her depth and serenity from the first and knew somehow that she was the right woman for me. "Woman" was the thing. Jane was a girl, and with her or thinking of her, I was a boy. Nell made me feel like that soberer thing, a man. She wasn't as strikingly pretty as Jane, but how lustrous a muted red her hair was, how it stirred in the breeze, how soft her pretty little hands were, how beautifully smooth her complexion was—and it was still that way sixty-three years later, when she was dying of cancer. Her voice calmed me. Like my mother, she spoke Southern Lady.

My only real reservation about Nell was her church. Baptist churches as I had known them in small Texas towns offered exhortative and elementary sermons, with music to match. I knew that First Baptist Church in downtown Amarillo was large and comparatively sophisticated, but when I visited there, I was always afraid the next person I met was going to ask, "Are you saved?" Nell never asked, of course, not that way. She knew my reservations. She had hers, too. Once, she quoted a line to me, "Yoke ye not with unbelievers." But she was not regretting, just musing—we were already yoked. After a few dates, I knew that Nell wasn't going to preach, and I'm sure she saw that I wasn't going to snort. Really, I had no impulse to do that. I envied and respected faith in her and in others, I just didn't like to be cornered. Wherever we went after we were married, we always found churches that suited both of us.

In Amarillo, I lived in a flophouse a mile or so from the paper, along with six or eight other single men, all of us in the same big room. Breakfast was part of the deal. Every morning, going to work, I picked up Jane, who had a room in a small, shabby house two doors farther south than mine and on the opposite side of Harrison Street, and then picked up Nell, who lived about the same distance north on the same street, upstairs in a nice, large house that belonged to a friend of her family. Neither of them had a car. The two of them had been friends, and they remained so, with reservations, as part of our triangle. One weekend I drove to a town north of Amarillo and met Jane's folks. Her father had owned a county-seat weekly paper until not long before I met him, so Jane had grown up with newspaper talk. She and her dad were very close. He didn't like me, I could tell. Maybe he wanted her to marry David, her classmate from the University of Colorado; I think she had been close to doing that when she and I met.

And I drove to the Osborne farm to meet Nell's parents. Her father was a powerful, dark-haired man who had a degree in history from Southern Methodist University but spoke Panhandle Farmer. I'm sure my untanned face and trained voice took him aback, though he was civil and even laughed at my jokes, a little. Nell's mother was quiet and warm, and at that meal she served two things I had missed badly during my time in the Northwest: black-eyed peas that had been picked green and home-canned, and pecan pie. Nell had coached her well.

A good many years later, Nell wrote some reminiscences of the war and postwar days in and around Panhandle. Some of the young men who had gone off to war came back to their farms. Not all did:

—The King Community, where I grew up, sent three young men into the service. One came home.

At the end of the war, Ben and Cora McGregor's son, Harry, was still listed as missing in action. The last time his parents and his younger brothers, Marvin and Bobby, saw him was when he buzzed the McGregors' farmhouse and, when his mother rushed out to see what was going on, flew low enough that she could recognize him.

He headed off toward Amarillo Army Air Base to get his plane refueled and serviced. The family "piled into the car," said Cora, and drove up to meet him as fast as they could. The men had already been on the way from the field after seeing that plane fly low over the house for the third time. His folks treasured the memory of that visit.

In 1955, I asked Cora if she thought Harry might still be alive, caught up in the machinery and confusion of war and its aftermath. "Oh, no," she said softly. "I'd know."

Then there were Nell's high school days, when she worked for a while as a typist for the Carson County clerk:

—At the courthouse, "Miss" Fannie Williams, the county clerk, and "Miss" Willie O'Neal could tell you who now owned that piece of land west of the railroad track and north of the Burum place. Miss Fannie could also tell you without checking who was getting married or had just been married. She had usually found out where the couple planned to live, where they'd be working. I don't know if she found out how many children they planned to have, but I wouldn't be surprised. All the while, she was campaigning, with her dimples and her beautiful white curls, as if the election was next Tuesday.

Miss Willie's typist, George, would be in a corner room in the clerk's office typing errorless copies of land transactions for The O'Neal Abstract

Company. Fannie and the lovely, well-groomed Faye
Granstaff would sit together proofreading recently
typed sheets for the big record books. They'd take
turns reading to each other, double-checking Section
2, Block 6 of whatever land survey it was to be sure
that piece of property was accurately identified. One
summer I had a job typing deeds and sales records
and oil leases onto those big sheets. I used a manual
typewriter with an oversized carriage. I got paid fifty
cents an hour and was delighted to be employed. At
lunchtime, I walked down to the Ramey Drug and
ate a ham sandwich and drank a Coke. Sometimes,
when I was feeling especially self-indulgent, I got
Jack or his sister, Ora Lee, to make me a chocolate
frozen malt. I don't think their mother usually
worked at the soda fountain.

At Mrs. Courage's grocery store, you could now
buy as many five-cent Hershey's as your mother
would allow. Nappy, who was black, or the other
male employee, who wore a ring in one ear to show
that he'd crossed the equator, would sack Mother's
groceries and carry them out to the car. New autos
were beginning to show up on the streets, and Dad
bought a car from Mrs. Franklin at the price she'd
set months ago when he'd asked her to order a Ford
for him when she could get it. He said he offered to
pay her the much higher price dealers in Amarillo
were demanding for those scarce new cars, but
she said a deal was a deal and she'd given him her
word. I think he bought his next three vehicles
from her before she retired from the dealership.

In September, the whole county came to
town one Saturday for the Fall Festival. A parade

down Main Street started things off. There'd be
kids riding decorated bicycles, antique cars and
tractors, the high school band, floats from civic
organizations and school groups. I remember
falling into the grease pit at the commercial garage
where my class was working on our float. Jim
Williams scrambled down to ask, "Are you hurt,
Nellie?" I said, "I'm okay, Jim," but I did let him
help me climb out. My jeans were filthy. I was
never a graceful child. The float was a real work of
art. It was a huge Southern-belle-type skirt. The
top part was that year's Fall Festival Queen, the
chocolate-box blonde, blue-eyed Juanita Mitchell,
her genuinely sweet, charming smile visible for
the whole route. The thing was mounted on
somebody's jeep, which was invisible except for a
slit for the driver to see through.

One special feature of every parade was the
manure spreader from Howard Lane's John Deere
house. He pulled it down the street with a tractor,
and it always bore a sign: "The only piece of
equipment we sell that we will not stand behind."

The horses and their riders were always last.
The men and women on horseback wore beautiful
riding outfits and brought out their best saddles.

At the pig barn, my mother ran into cheerful,
friendly Elizabeth Homen, who would shout over
the racket, "Vell, Missis Osborne! Ve only meet at
pig shows!" Daniel Homen and his brothers and
my brothers, Jim and David, would be showing
pigs. The barn reeked of Chester Whites and the
baby powder rubbed into their hides to make them
whiter yet. Mrs. Homen was right. They were both

busy ladies, and they went to different churches,
so they didn't see each other, even on Sundays.
Elizabeth Homen was probably second-generation
American. Her delightful Polish lilt could be heard
in every word. There was never a better woman or a
better citizen.

After ten months on the Amarillo paper, restless again and
also feeling the need of space and time to think things over, I
wrote the *Fort Worth Star-Telegram* and went for an interview.
The editor, John Ellis, small and sixtyish, had seen clippings of
some of my news stories. "You're plumb pro," he said, "I think
you can come on down." That was as formal an offer as I ever got,
but I took it. By the time I had gone to work at the *Star-Telegram*,
in the early summer of 1956, I was sure I loved Nell and wanted
her for my wife. I hadn't proposed to her, though, and was still
dating Jane, too—or was until she became ill and left the *Globe-
News* to stay with friends at Junction, in the Texas Hill Country.
I went to Fort Worth uncommitted. Then the letters started. If
I needed assurance about Nell's mind and spirit, it came in her
style, which was simple, warm, and often casually witty. It is
with great shame that I admit this: with a couple of exceptions,
I didn't keep her letters. How could I have been so dull, so crass,
so lacking in foresight? We wrote each other almost every day,
and she, as I found out later, kept my letters. With all their silli-
ness and shallowness, they're in the strong box at the bank, in
the original envelopes. One of hers that I can come fairly close
to reconstructing came when I had driven to Junction to tell Jane
goodbye. Nell, it developed, had tried to phone me. He's gone to
Junction, someone told her. Nell assumed that I had gone there
to propose to Jane. She wrote, approximately, "When they told
me, I thought, 'Oh, why has he done that? Why have things
turned out this way? Why?...Never mind. I wish you the best

in everything. Love, Nell." Breaking off with Jane was probably the hardest thing I've ever done. It left me unspeakably sad and profoundly relieved. On the long, late-night drive back to Fort Worth afterward I did what I had always thought people did only in books: I cried and laughed at the same time.

When I got off work that Monday afternoon and found Nell's letter, I phoned her—told her why I had gone to Junction and what I had done and asked if I could come and see her the next weekend. South of Amarillo on that Saturday night, we stood outside the car on hard plains ground, because I thought stars and fresh air were the right setting for the occasion, and I said quietly, not pleading and not demanding, "Marry me, Nell." She said, "All right." We were in each other's arms immediately, of course. But the words were in the tone of our next sixty-two-and-a-half years. Gushiness was not for us; we knew what we meant. We were married in October at her home on the farm, with the Baptist preacher from Panhandle presiding. When I had kissed my bride and turned toward the few guests, I saw tears in Dad's eyes.

Neither Nell nor I ever looked at ease in photographs. She had sent a studio picture of herself to me in Fort Worth, and I had sent it on to my folks in California. It was a truly awful picture, stern and charmless. I know my folks were appalled, though Mother's only comment was, "She has pretty hands." (That, she did, even when she was in her eighties and arthritis had skewed her right thumb into an impossible angle.) A few days later, my folks received a letter from her. It was so warm and mature, so generous and ladylike, so casually literate, that it cleared away all their doubts. And when Nell met my folks' plane at Amarillo before the wedding—I was on the way, driving from Fort Worth—Dad, bless him, said, "You're positively beautiful!" We spent our wedding night in a Lubbock motel and drove to Fort Worth the next day.

I had rented a house for us on the remnant of a ranch just west of town. It had been a ranch hand's house before. I told Nell it was in a beautiful setting and very clean. When we got there and stepped inside, she looked around, unpacked, put on jeans, got onto her knees, and started scrubbing the floor. Well, at least I was right about the setting. There were nice small oaks and a long, narrow pond with reasonably clear water. Mrs. Allen, who lived on the place, had a flock of ugly Muscovy ducks. She was very proud of them, as we learned when she reported at about the end of our first year there that with her outside listening device the night before, she had heard a duck being murdered by our barely grown Airedale, Maggie. We were sorry; we tried everything we knew to confine Maggie. She was an Airedale Houdini, squirming or bursting out of all collars. We couldn't keep her shut up in the house, because our son, Andrew, was at the crawling stage.

Maggie killed at least one more duck. I got an idea. I called the director of the Forest Park Zoo, Lawrence Curtis, whom the *Star-Telegram's* popular writer, George Dolan, often twitted engagingly in his column. The zoo had a large flock of Muscovy ducks, all of which looked to me exactly like the ones in Mrs. Allen's flock. I asked Curtis could I... Sure, he said, he would lend me a long-handled net. If anyone questioned me, I should say I was doing something for him. But I wondered: if I put an undocumented duck into Mrs. Allen's flock, would she recognize it as an intruder? We never found out, because we turned up a duckless house we liked and moved to it. I took the net back to Curtis.

We moved twice more during our seven Fort Worth years. The last house, finally, had air conditioning. There were four of us for most of those years, Elizabeth having come along in 1959. On the evening *Star-Telegram*, I had started, as usual, on the police beat. Along with the competing *Fort Worth Press's*

fine reporter Harold Williams and, often, the mellow-voiced
WBAP radio reporter, Wayne Brown, I sat in the press room at
the police station most of the time and did my reporting main-
ly by phone. Harold and I, like other police reporters from the
two papers, shared routine information such as names and ages.
Otherwise, we would unnecessarily pester the pimps and pros-
titutes who were involved in, or witnesses to, most Fort Worth
murders. Those people surprisingly often answered our ques-
tions. Maybe they enjoyed the publicity.

One day, though, when there had been an uncommonly in-
teresting murder, neither Harold nor I could get at anyone with
the details we needed. The central prostitute refused to come to
the phone. Deadline was approaching. In those days, there was
no caller ID, and I tried something. In my best whoremonger
voice, I ordered the man who answered, "Lemme tawk to Sal-
ly. Tell her it's Don cawlin'." When Sally came to the phone, I
immediately identified myself, as ethics required, and told her I
was with the *Star-Telegram*. She must have figured I had tricked
her fair and square. She answered all my questions, and I got
the details for my story. Poor Harold, just across the small room,
heard everything except the answers. He knew that this time, I
was keeping those to myself, and he understood my doing so. I
think he tried the same trick, but Sally was tired of that game.
She wouldn't talk to him.

Sally, by the way, was white. All, or practically all, the sizable
police stories that got into the *Star-Telegram* in those days were
about white people, or at least white victims. A black-on-black
murder got maybe three paragraphs. In a *Wichita Eagle* column
of mine, written when I had much more detailed memories of the
fifties and sixties than I now have, I recalled that the *Star-Tele-
gram*, like other Texas newspapers, would not call a black woman
"Mrs." So we wrote, "The Jones woman." We did not run pictures
of black brides or, as a rule, obituaries of black people:

—Black people were usually identified as such
unless their addresses, given in the stories, were
clearly in the black part of town. Because of that
practice, I once had to ask a man on the phone,
"Are you a Negro, sir?" It was an uncomfortable
task, no matter which way the answer came back.
A white man might have shown anger at being
asked—not because color had nothing to do with
the story but because he considered it an insult
to be taken for a Negro. A black man, though he
might have felt the same about being taken for a
white man, would not likely have lost his temper
but could, instead, have withered me with a
pointed stateliness. In this case, the man must have
recognized the reluctance in my voice. His answer
was mercifully straightforward: "Yes sir."

When I had spent about three months on the police beat,
I was put on the city desk as a rewriteman. That meant tak-
ing phone calls from reporters who either dictated stories to me
off the tops of their heads or gave me notes that I turned into
stories. The deadline for our first edition was, I think, 11:30
a.m., so there wasn't time for a reporter to come in from a city
council meeting or a house fire and eliminate the middleman,
me. I fitted the phone hook onto my left shoulder and rattled
a manual typewriter that was loaded with a sandwich of two
sheets of copy paper and one sheet, between, of carbon paper.
When a reporter dictated, I edited as I typed, fixing grammar,
tightening sentences, trying to avoid journalese. I never had re-
porters gripe at me afterward for changing things. Maybe they
didn't notice—they had composed into the air and under fire,
after all. I liked the work, and once in a while I got the chance
to do a story on my own. That first summer, when I had gone to

the office on a Sunday morning as usual to read the paper rather than spend a quarter for one, the phone rang. Since there was no afternoon paper that day, I was the only person in the newsroom. It's remarkable to think, now, that anyone who wanted could have come in off the street as I had and climbed the stairs to where reporters' notes on pending stories were lying on desks everywhere. It was the editor, John Ellis, on the phone. He told me there had been a gas explosion near Dumas, in the Panhandle. Get going, he said. I flew to Amarillo, drove a rented car to the scene, wrote my story, phoned it in for the Monday morning paper, drove back to Amarillo, and went out with Nell.

The city editor of the afternoon paper when I started at the *Star-Telegram* was Charles K. Boatner, a shambling man in probably his late forties. Though charm was not a factor in his effectiveness, he was always pleasant to me, and he knew both news values and English grammar. I remarked to him, early in my rewriting days, that a certain reporter wrote well. Charley wrinkled his nose. "He puts a singular verb to a plural subject," he said. I checked the carbon copy of the reporter's next story; it was true.

English usage concerned all of us on the staff. After the second-edition deadline of 1:00 or 1:30 p.m., I often had lunch across the street at the Worth Hotel with John Mort, who covered city hall, and we would talk the Associated Press stylebook and *Fowler's Modern English Usage*, along with Waugh and Nabokov, both of whom John had read and I had not. John was three or four years older than I and was a war veteran, though, like so many others, he almost never spoke about his battle experiences. John had been a boxer in college. He was short, but his shoulders were broad enough to add a lot to his reach. To me he seemed urbane and experienced. He knew French; he read everything; he was as bitingly skeptical as Captain Yossarian in *Catch 22*—which I'm sure he had read, though I hadn't. He was married to Sarah. Her father was the editor, whose office and person John therefore took care never to be seen near or with.

All of us except John called the editor Mr. Ellis, even among ourselves. John called him "The Mouse." On the infrequent occasions when Mr. Ellis had emerged from his office and stepped into the newsroom, John would report, "The Mouse came out of his hole." In my last couple of years in Fort Worth, we lived in a nice house whose backyard backed up to the Morts'. They had a Great Dane named Charles (for Boatner? I don't think I ever asked) and a pet, anonymous, raccoon. The raccoon had a little house in the backyard, and when a norther came in at night, it would get out of bed, turn the house around so the cold wind wouldn't come in through the door, and go back to sleep.

John worked in his yard a lot. I mowed our lawn, nothing more, and that only when I had to. Once, when John and I were standing outside my house, I pointed to a clump of grass in the lawn and asked him what kind it was.

"That," he said, with horror, "is crab grass."

Nature in general, though, wasn't an interest of his. Another time when we were talking outside, I cocked an ear toward a tree and said those were nice dove songs, weren't they?

"Is that what they are?" John said. "I always thought those were little owls."

The *Star-Telegram* years taught me much about newspaper work and about Fort Worth. I came to think I knew every street in town. That was when Boatner had gone off to serve in the presidential campaign of Lyndon Johnson and I had become assistant city editor of the evening paper. The new city editor, Jack Douglas, a war veteran, was missing parts of two fingers—he never said why, but I would bet he had grabbed a live grenade and thrown it away not quite in time. Jack, who grew up in Albany, Texas, was farm-boy funny, with a streak of orneriness. He had an endless supply of often endless stories from his youth, and he liked to start one when he saw that I was furiously at work, on deadline. He would lean back in his swivel chair, take his pipe out of his mouth, and begin, "There in Albany..." I ignored him at such times, but I remember how one of his stories about his boyhood in Albany began:

"I attended a train wreck once, and the conductor was lying there with a bolt through his head, dead. Well, we looked around, seeing what else we could find,..."

Jack was maybe forty, blond, short, and very broad, a powerful man. He found out one day what John Mort called him: "Stubby." That was OK, Jack said, "if it refers to my stature, and not my disability." Sometimes Mort brought his lunch to work. He left it on his desk during the morning with the top of the brown paper sack not folded down but twisted—so it wouldn't look like what it was, as he admitted. One day when John was out of the room, Jack went over to his desk and rolled the sack the usual lunch-sack way. He stuck a note on it. "Let's face it," it said, "you're poor." When John came back and read the note, he actually laughed. I think it was the only time I saw him do that in my seven years on the paper.

When I got off a crack he liked, he would wheel around with his back to me so I wouldn't see him smile. Sometimes the crack was such as would be unforgivably racist today, so much so that I would have to apologize on television and resign as CEO or governor or whatever. John was a liberal. So were, I'm sure, most of the reporters and editors—except for me. Still, nearly all of them made and laughed at such jokes. Nearly all, I think, accepted "separate but equal" procedures in the schools. I know I did. Sixty years ago, that was Texas. I have become moderately sensitized, maybe civilized, since then. So it seems to me, but Kamala Harris would disagree.

Being part of the dominant and, we thought, superior race was so easy and natural that it seems frightening to think about it. I was not taught in childhood that black people were different. I didn't have to be—it was obvious to anybody. What I was taught was that Negroes were inferior. All of us, at least in small Texas towns, were taught that. My family, and many others, nonetheless treated black people with what we thought was courtesy, even affection. The affection was condescending, of course, and it must have been resentfully recognized as such. Think lord and knave in Shakespeare's time; think colonial officer and dark-skinned Calcuttan in the days of the British Empire. We were the ruling race, and we behaved accordingly. Deep shame on us. Still, some of today's accepted attitudes toward race seem to me to be harmful, too, albeit better intentioned than the old ways were. At the same time, I recognize that such opinions often rise from generosity and empathy, traits that too many conservatives are short on.

At the *Star-Telegram*, I broke one story. It wasn't big, but it was exclusive for the moment. On the day Alaska was admitted as a state, January 3, 1959, it occurred to me that the official state song, "Texas, Our Texas," which every school kid in Texas had to memorize, was now wrong, because a line said, "Largest and grandest." I phoned William Marsh, the Fort Worth composer who had set the lyrics to music. The problem hadn't occurred to him. "That does take the wind out of my sails," he said, and soon he changed the invalidated word to "boldest." I wrote a small story about the change, thinking it would surely win first prize in the annual Texas AP Managing Editors' contest for short features. The story came out on Page 1 with this headline: "Marsh Sails Are Windless." Who, glancing, would guess what the story was about? And there went my prize. Maybe I wouldn't have won, anyway, but I was disappointed and angry. It was not the only time in my career that I was angry at a copy editor.

The biggest story I did for the *Star-Telegram* came on September 30, 1962. The Van Cliburn International Piano Competition, named for a young Fort Worth virtuoso, was about to have its premiere, and I, since I knew something about classical music, was assigned to cover the proceedings. I wrote a story or two, having interviewed the self-effacing Cliburn and his over-bearing mother, and then suddenly got reassigned. A young man named James Meredith was about to be admitted to the University of Mississippi as its first black student, and a large protest was expected.

When I got there, several hundred students had already gathered, yelling, in The Grove, outside the administrative building called The Lyceum. One, a man of probably gradu-ate-student age, jumped onto I forget what sort of platform and harangued the crowd. "There's a marshal up in the Lyceum, dead," he said, "and it's not worth it for a damn Nigger." Voices, unbelieving, began shouting back at him. "What are you trying to tell us, John?" (Or whatever his name was. All of this is from memory; if I kept a copy of my story, I can't find it.) I had to find out about the marshal. I edged through the crowd and up to the Lyceum. There, an AP reporter was at a teletype, shirtless, punching away with pinpoints of blood on his back, obviously from birdshot.

The word about the marshal was wrong, I found out, but a foreign reporter had been killed outside, in bushes behind the Lyceum. I had to get to the funeral home and confirm that and also find a phone so I could call in my story. I wasn't fool enough to go back where the reporter had been killed. The only way was straight through the crowd of yelling students. As I walked across the open space between the building and the crowd, someone shouted, "Who's that walking?" Several came up to me, and one demanded to know who I was. I was very glad I could say I was with the *Fort Worth Star-Telegram* and not *The New York Times*. They let me pass.

In the funeral home, a young, large, strikingly handsome

auburn-haired man lay dead. Another man, plump and mus-
tached, came in just then, took one look, said "It's Paul," and
rushed across the room to use the phone. He and the dead man
were with Agence France-Presse. I left, found a phone booth,
and called the *Star-Telegram*. Make it first-person, I was told,
and I dictated for an hour and a half, up till the 1:30 a.m. dead-
line. I do remember the lead of my story:

> The battle that began after the battle was over was
> almost like a genuine wartime military engagement.
> I stood in the midst of both sides at various times
> during the night and saw men wounded, bleeding
> and dead.

The editors should by all means have deleted either "war-
time" or "military," and really, there wasn't much excuse for a
first-person approach. Nonetheless, the story won first prize in
the spot-news category of the next Texas AP Managing Editors'
contest. That was nice, and still I wasn't writing what I really
craved to write, not that I knew exactly what that was. Some-
thing that might end up between solider covers than newspaper
pages, I knew that much. At one point, I took a six-month leave
from the *Star-Telegram* so the four of us could go to Mexico and
live cheaply while I wrote and wrote. The Mexico part didn't
last. The kids got sick, and we were afraid to stay longer. We
went to Amarillo instead, and I've kept barely a scrap of such
writing as I turned out during that leave. Juvenilia, it all was,
though I was past thirty by then.

VI.

In Fort Worth, if I touched a shoe to a single blade of grass, chiggers would make itchy scales up and down my shins. In my part of the Panhandle, as yet, chiggers don't exist. If global warming brings them here, I'm off to Colorado, or Greenland. In Fort Worth, if I accidentally bit myself while eating or sleeping, I was sure to develop a canker sore that caused not only a painful lump in my mouth but also symptoms much like flu. I still get a canker sore when I bite myself, but at least the illness has gone away. Chiggers and canker sores, together with the draining summer heat, together with my growing awareness of advertisers' influence on the *Star-Telegram*'s news decisions, together with my chronic restlessness, finally put an end to what I have since realized was a valuable seven-year introduction to newspaper life and, in fact, life.

As assistant city editor of the evening *Star-Telegram* I had twice run the city side alone for six weeks while Jack Douglas, who succeeded Boatner as city editor, was attending editors' seminars or on vacation. I think I was generally respected by the news staff on the *Star-Telegram*. By the wheels, too, but it took some indulgence on their part. In my later years at the paper, I sat across a desk from the associate editor, Bert Griffith, a bald, genial man in probably his late sixties who when I started work there had been the salty and, I think, very capable news editor. He and I joked and grumbled together across the desk. When I saw something about the paper that offended me, though, I would slam my copy down on the desk. "This is a sorry paper," I said on a good many occasions. Finally, in the summer of 1963, I said it one too many times. Griff, as we all called him, said in exasperation, "Well, then, why don't you quit?"

"I am quitting," I said. "I put in my application to the AP a couple of weeks ago."

Griff got up without a word and strode back to the editor's office, where, to judge by his haste, they may have been planning to make some different use of me. So? Though I somewhat regret having been inconsiderate of Griff's loyalty to the paper, I do not regret the loss of whatever new assignment may have been in the wind. I had already told myself that if I should end up as editor of the *Star-Telegram*, I would consider my life to have been wasted. I still feel that way. The same if I had carried out Leff's assessment of my potentiality and become a rich and famous *Lieder* singer. What a life that would have been, always on an airplane, always under pressure, never having a real home and family. I did have a home and family, wonderful ones. At home, I helped Nell minimally while she raised our two pre-school children and kept house. Also at home, I vocalized and learned Schubert and Schumann and Fauré songs for, probably, two hours most days. In Fort Worth, I was studying with Arlene Sollenberger, who saw right away that I was not truly a baritone and taught me the vowel shadings necessary to handle a tenor's high tones and high tessituras. I gave a recital of art songs at her house, and eight or ten of my newsroom friends, including Mort, Griffith, and Douglas, attended and gamely stayed awake.

But then we moved to Denver, where summers were much cooler and there were no chiggers and where, almost incidentally, I had taken a job as an editor with The Associated Press. Naturally I went back to Leff. We worked for several months, and finally one day she leaned back from the piano and said, "Now it can be told. I had despaired of your ever singing well again." My technique had slipped that badly without my knowing it. Like many singers, I needed a full-time teacher. No; I needed Eleanor Leffingwell full-time. She, as I found by studying with a dozen others over many years and many moves, was the only one who could keep my production free. I had been deceiving the others, along with myself, into thinking I knew how to sing.

During the year and a half that I worked for the AP, I took coaching lessons at the University of Colorado from Aksel Schiøtz, who in early mid-career had lost control of one side of his face after an operation to remove a tumor from his acoustic nerve. He still sang some, now as a baritone, but except for marvelously resonant low notes was far from the singer he had been. As a coach, I'm afraid, he believed in *laissez-faire;* or it may have been a kind of respect, a decision that at my age I was singing a certain way and shouldn't be nudged into another. He taught me very little. With the technique that Leff had reawakened in me, I sang well enough to represent Colorado at a regional or perhaps national convention in Austin of the National Association of Teachers of Singing, where I sang "Il mio tesoro" from Mozart's *Don Giovanni.* At that time, and for years afterward, I took the long cadenza in that aria on one breath, with a *ritardando* at the end. No more. Old singers lose lung capacity even more commonly than tonal steadiness—both of which I lost for years but for the last three years, concentrating on technique more than ever before, have tried to regain in part, or else to conceal. When the aging Lotte Lehmann, on a record, sings the song "An die Musik," she grabs breaths almost imperceptibly at several places where Schubert hadn't really made room for a breath. That is artistry and also technique, and most admirable. Really, though, it's better to have air.

People hear a good singer and say, "A beautiful voice." What they hear, though, is not necessarily that but simply skill at letting the voice be itself. A natural instrument helps, of course, but everyone has enough of that to be a fine singer, given a decent ear and good training. A voice is an instrument, like a violin. Learning to play it right is tricky because we have been playing it since birth. Doing so is automatic, and the components, the tongues and palates and diaphragms, are invisible. Furthermore, singers do not hear themselves as violinists or clarinetists do, though they usually think they do. What sounds to an untrained singer like a "rich" tone is probably a throaty, held-back sound that lacks the resonance, the "ping," that gives a voice conviction, carrying power, and beauty. Learning to sing right means learning not to interfere with the voice, which means teaching each small part of the inner, unseen mechanism to lie back and not try to make tone. I have reminded myself of that for several years, and now, finally, am able to think of singing somewhat in public again. What I mean is that I am working on a demanding song cycle—Beethoven's wonderful *An die ferne Geliebte* (To the Distant Beloved)—and am hoping to get it into decent enough shape to make a CD, with piano, for the possible use of my children and grandchildren. It won't be perfect, I'm sure. I hope it will be good enough for a descendant to say to a friend, "Listen to what Great-Granddad did when he was a ninety-two-year-old tenor." If not, I will have had the pleasure of living in the nucleus of a great work as only a performing singer or instrumentalist can do.

Partly because I spent so much time vocalizing and studying songs, I did very little writing except for newspaper prose for forty years and more. Was that smart of me? I've never decided. Singing is a deep pleasure, even when it's not done right. It cools the day's tensions like the headwaters of the Danube. A song in your head, even if it's "Mairzy Doats," is like a gyroscope that stabilizes your nerves while your fingers tap out accounts of murders and corruption. Singing does much for you, but the trouble is, it doesn't last. It's not on paper, and unless you're a pro, it's not on a commercial disc or YouTube. When your lungs wither and your vocal cords turn to emery sticks, you're probably done. I'm trying not to be done. We shall see.

I try to imagine that I had never sung but had written instead, those two hours a day for forty years and more. Would I have produced books worth keeping? Maybe not, especially after full days of writing at work. I know this: I would have allowed Nell and our kids a chance to listen to something else than my voice, sometimes to make their own kinds of noise. Bless them, they were patient and indulgent; they didn't shush me, didn't run out of the room with fingers in their ears. And Nell knew very well how much singing meant to me. After retirement, when I hadn't realized how badly my technique had slipped, a choir director told me that the excessive vibrato of my voice was throwing the other singers off. They couldn't tell what note I was singing. I must have sounded somewhat like a baritone of the 1950s, about whom, when we heard him on the radio, Dad said, "He's shooting at those notes scatterbore and not always hitting them." I wrote a poem that in opaque terms said farewell to my voice. Nell read it, understood it instantly, and threw her arms around me, sobbing in love and sympathy.

Except for one thing, our year-and-a-half in Denver was delightful. Our kids were three-and-a-half and five years old at the start: enchanting ages. They hiked in the foothills with me and sledded on a grassy hill near Golden. Betsy, as we always called her—she's Elizabeth to everybody else, these days—skied for hours in the level backyard, even when the snow was a mini-archipelago with grass between islands and her skis were toys with mere toe straps, as rudimentary as the kiddie car I had owned at that age. Both kids listened raptly when I read to them, and when, in an Edward Lear poem, I got to the line, "You runcible goose!" Andy fell off the couch laughing. They and Nell and I went on beautiful mountain drives. From a ditch next to our house in

Lakewood we harvested wild asparagus spears, as thin as match sticks and utterly ravishing. (One of the trials of my present decade is that my diet forbids me to eat asparagus.) I skied a lot and did a little fly fishing, and sometimes I hiked with Bob, who was living in Fort Collins with his wife and four children.

The one big drawback to the Denver stay was that the AP put me on the overnight shift. I saw far too little of my family with that schedule, and I didn't sleep well. True, in the winter when I would get home in the dark hours of morning and step into Betsy's room, just to make sure she was all right, she would come instantly awake and jump up in bed for a hug. So of course that became an unfailing routine of mine. And we acquired a puppy, another Airedale, which we named Alec. He became the best and funniest dog you could imagine, amiable, intelligent, and, as I'll explain later, superstitious. He was another of the many pleasures for us in those years of 1963 to 1965. They weren't quite enough.

I always followed the help-wanted ads in *Editor & Publisher* magazine, just in case. One day there was one from the *Globe-News*: an opening for a rewriteman. Amarillo! The town and the paper where Nell and I met; the plains we both loved; in short, home. We went, I with the understanding that I would work only half-days so I could go home and write the poetry and fiction I had always longed to write. That schedule lasted two or three months, producing not a single masterpiece. Then the city editor left, and I was given the job. It was one of the best I ever had, and it didn't hurt that it was in the city I loved best, that the children were still at delightful ages, that Nell and I were young and healthy, and that we found a rambling old house we loved in a pretty neighborhood in the west part of town.

Sam Houston Park was two or three houses away. The children, six and seven years old when we arrived in Amarillo, walked there alone to play alone—it was that different a time, 1965. The house had an unfinished atticlike room, and in that room, once, we hung up a goose that Felix Phillips, the outdoor editor at the paper, had shot and given us. Leave it there three days before you cook it, he advised us. On one of those days, Alec, our Airedale, wandered into the room, nudged the goose with his muzzle, and was bumped lightly on the return swing. He scrabbled out of the room backwards, and thereafter could never be persuaded to go back into that room. A superstitious dog, and part of the family.

After three fine years, I figured out a way to make a living and still have time for writing. I would go back to college, finish a degree from where I had left off, the middle of my junior year, then get a master's, and then teach college English, writing all through the free summers and also finding more time and less pressure during the academic year than I told myself I had as a newspaperman. In September 1968, we moved to Lubbock. I got the B.A. from Texas Tech University in a year and the M.A. in another year, with no memorable events except the classes in medieval literature under Dr. Beverly Gilbert, a brilliant and enthusiastic young Amarillo woman who became a warm friend of Nell's and mine. Well, there was a memorable event. It did not reflect well on Tech or, in fact, the sensitivity of university professors of English. In a course on English Romantic poetry, we read Kipling's "Danny Deever," about a young British soldier who "shot a comrade sleepin'" and to the horror and grief of his companions is about to be hanged in front of the assembled regiment:

"What makes the rear-rank breathe so 'ard?" said Files-on-Parade.

"It's bitter cold, it's bitter cold," the Color-Sergeant said.

"What makes that front-rank man fall down?" said Files-on-Parade.

"A touch o' sun, a touch o' sun," the Color-Sergeant said.

Those lines baffled one of my fellow students. She asked the teacher (not Beverly Gilbert) to explain it. The teacher was baffled, too, but had a suggestion. "Peculiarity of the local climate," she said with a shrug. Since then, that line has served Nell, the kids, and me as a handy explanation for all sorts of puzzling events. Why did my computer keep repeating the letter *o* when I had only touched it once? "Peculiarity of the local climate."

Back to the Panhandle then, to what was then West Texas State University, where I groaned through two years of the worst and hardest job I ever had, teaching five sections of freshman composition to students most of whom, poor kids, had seldom read a book that wasn't assigned and who were taking the course only because it was required. "My experiences with books is very seldom," they wrote, and, in a theme about *The Importance of Being Earnest,* "When they hear this, the girls sull up and go in the house," and, my favorite and my dad's, "What Shakespeare is trying to say..." Most of my students wrote about "alot" of such and such, and they thought the word "prodigal," in the Bible story, meant wandering.

I had no idea how to teach such classes. I didn't teach, really, I edited—marked every misspelling, every incoherency, everything I would have changed on a reporter's copy, not that I had often seen a reporter's copy as misspelled and incoherent as most of the essays my students turned in. On the evaluations students made at semesters' ends, one young man wrote, "Just too damn hard." He was right. If, God forbid, I were teaching those courses again, I would start with at least two weeks of sounds of letters, of parts of speech, of lay-laid-laids and lie-lay-lains—of the things I had been taught in the fourth grade—and I would force myself not to mark small, everyday errors. Maybe that way I would last more than two years. As it was, I perceived that I was condemned to teach freshman comp for the rest of my career unless I got a doctorate, and so in the fall of 1972 we were off to Austin and the University of Texas.

Good judgment about salability, whether of my writings or my abilities, has never been a quality of mine, any more than it was of my dad's. In English class at Colorado Springs, I had been introduced to *Beowulf* by a sweet and able teacher who reminded me of my mother's maiden aunts. Her name, I think, was Skidmore. When she had read aloud Beowulf's detailed speech about his many feats of heroism and got to the line, "Not that I boast of it," she looked up at us and said, "Oh, no!" Our book had, I think, just one sample of the original Old English. It was about a ship voyage:

> Gewat tha ofer waegholm,
> winde gefysed,
> Flota famigheals,
> fugle gelicost

and was ably translated in the book as:

> "Went then oer the wave-sea,
> by the wind favored,
> The floater foamy-necked,
> to a fowl likest."

I was charmed by what I supposed the sound of the Old English was, and when I arrived in Austin it was *Beowulf* that I chose as my doctoral subject. That of course greatly narrowed my choices of future employment, which were already limited by the facts that I was forty-four years old when I finished and was— sorry, but this was a handicap, as it would be today—a white male. As I say, my judgment was poor. I should have chosen Frost or maybe Marjorie Kinnan Rawlings, whose style in *The Yearling* charmed me at twelve and has been a model to me since.

I did my research and writing as the first product of a *Doktorvater* much younger than I, Thomas Cable, who was already on his way to professional esteem and as much fame as a philologist and Old English prosodist can ever expect to have. He, especially, and almost all the rest of the graduate faculty, impressed me with their scholarship and, what is more, common sense. I finished my Ph.D. in Beowulfian prosody in two years, writing a dissertation much of which now seems incomprehensible to me. They were good years for me, mainly because Nell did everything except my UT work. One sad event: poor Alec, the Airedale, terrified by the firecrackers on New Year's Eve, broke through the backyard fence and vanished. We never found him.

I looked for a teaching job, found nothing in my specialty, but, having the necessary "terminal degree" to show on the record—no matter that Beowulf never went near a newsroom—used that and my former career to get a job teaching journalism at South Dakota State University. Off we went again. Poor Nell.

Students become journalism majors because they want to be journalists and usually because they want to learn to write. Teaching them, compared to teaching freshman comp, was a snap and almost a joy. At SDSU, I had solid, pleasant, generally hard-working students. One of them was a young man from a small town where the old folks still spoke German. He wrote correctly but stiffly, and when I reminded him of the precept, Write the Way You Talk, he said, "But Dr. Williams, that is the way I talk." It was, all right, but he worked so hard and loosened up so much that I gave him an A for the semester. As a reporting exercise one day, I told the class about the students' demonstration—riot, really—at Ole Miss when James Meredith was admitted. Now write a news story about it, I told them. Afterward, when I looked through the stories, I found that every student had assumed that the demonstration was not against, but for, Meredith's admission. The North was that different from the South then. It may still be.

Our two years in Brookings were pleasant but uneventful, unless northern winters count as events. One night there was a knock on our door, and a man walking with four or five teenage boys said they were cold, and could they come in? They could, of course, and I think the request was routinely made and granted in a South Dakota winter. One night, when the SDSU car I was using had slid into a snowbank across the street from our house, I tried for a bitter hour with Andy, my son, to dig it out, but when I started the engine, the tires just spun. The temperature was twenty-seven below zero. We were suffering; we gave up. When I tried again, a half hour later, the car backed out easily—because, Andy figures, the ice and snow had been melted by the hot tires at first and had then refrozen, providing some traction since we had shoveled the snow away. I think that experience, as much as anything, made him what he is today, a confirmed Houstonian, hostile to the mere thought of freezing weather. One winter day, it actually got warm enough to thaw the puddles on the sidewalk at the college. I splashed through them with childish joy. Except for the winters, though, and the accent, that part of South Dakota was close kin to the Texas Panhandle, people and all.

Ah, but it wasn't Texas. It didn't have bluebonnets, or the Alamo, or shrimp tacos. Or, of course, siblings, parents, and childhood memories. I took a job teaching journalism at Baylor University, where the department head was Loyal Gould, a former newspaper and television reporter who had worked at the *Globe-News*, though not when I was there. From cold Brookings we went to hot Waco. It was only fourteen miles from McGregor, where I had spent two childhood years during the Depression. Through his book *Texas Wild* I made a friend who lived there: Richard Phelan, whose aphoristic and often biting perceptions of books and life stimulated, enlightened, and amused me by mail and e-mail for a quarter century. Samples:

—When I see reporters ask lottery winners what
they will do with their millions, I daydream about
the answer I would give. I would say, "I am going

to buy five thousand dollars' worth of books that I have always wanted and move to some city high in tropical mountains (where you get the best climate in the world) and live there and read them." Oaxaca is such a city. But of course I don't buy lottery tickets.

—(On being disappointed by single-author books of poems:) It turns out that even the most gifted writers produce only a few top-drawer poems, and they are, of course, in the anthologies.

—I have decided that Mozart's clarinet concerto should be transcribed into a piano concerto. The music is beautiful, but thirty-five minutes of clarinet is like eating six desserts in a row.

—It seems unlikely that my respectful reading of *The Aeneid* will make me a better or wiser person. I'm nearly through. What has kept me going is the thought, "I'm reading a great classic." Occasionally some human relationship actually interests me for a few pages; then it lapses back to ridiculous religion and superstition, impossible achievements in battle, and Greek and Latin name-strewing.

—(June 2007) John Graves has indeed kept writing when he no longer had anything to say. I bought his most recent book and wish I hadn't. The blame may lie with editors, hoping for another success from an author who hasn't one in him.

—A brochure from Prescott College says Dr. Larry Strom "completed his contract with earthly life" recently. I wonder who signed that document. Dr. Strom, no doubt, but who was the signatory of the second part?

Dick had worked for *Sports Illustrated*, covering I think mostly tennis and golf. One assignment was to do a story on sports in Newfoundland and Greenland.

> —My photographer and I went up in an old plane that had been worn out in the Berlin airlift. On takeoff from an air base in New Jersey, the pilot slammed on the brakes and the young corporal who did the job of stewardess said, with a tight smile and in an adolescent voice, "Please abandon the aircraft. The aircraft is on fire." They put the fire out (it was in an engine), and we continued. . . . In Newfoundland, the aurora filled the whole sky with slow-moving, dull colors. I was disappointed in it. . . . I actually have a screen saver titled Aurora. . . . [It] is as boring as nature's.

Though Dick and I differed in political philosophy, religion, and (I'm sure) sexual orientation, we found plenty of material for comment in books, public figures, manners, and nature. I admired his worldliness and wit somewhat as I had John Mort's at the *Star-Telegram*. And Dick, for all his scoffing, could be touched by everyday goodness. He wrote me this about a truck-driving neighbor:

> —[H]e is one of the most honest, decent, responsible people I have known. He put his pay checks in the bank for his wife to spend, and when she divorced him, he agreed to take over all the credit-card debt—$40,000—because he knew that if he didn't, she would lose their second-mortgaged house; and he wanted his children to grow up in the house they had always lived in. He uses a fan instead of air conditioning in the summer, and blankets instead of heat in the winter (when he's at

home), because while paying off the credit cards
he's putting away money to buy his daughter her
first car when she turns sixteen. I have lent him
small amounts of money and I don't keep track. I
know he'll hand me fifty dollars a payday till it's
paid back.

For his last year or so, Dick had abdominal pain from what
I suspect was cancer, though he never said so. He e-mailed me
this on March 17, 2009:

—The stomach pain is better, a little. I expected
my doctor to call me in yesterday for some exam
(not an MRI), but he didn't. He just prescribed
a medication for stomach pain and apparently
decided the exam could wait until the pills either
work or don't.

—Right now I'm listening to a fine performance
of the New World Symphony, all harmonies and
melodies. This afternoon I played the Bruch violin
concerto. Good for bellyache.

That was all, and the next morning he went across the
street, lay down on the grass, and shot himself. He had told me
he would do that rather than go into a nursing home, but his
"bellyache" may just as well have been the reason. His body was
cremated, and friends of Dick's did as this scoffing atheist had
asked: they sifted his ashes into a field of gorgeous Texas blue-
bonnets. A few weeks later, with a possible *Letters of R.C. Phelan*
in mind, I put together a manuscript of comments that Dick
had sent to me and to his and my writer friend Elroy Bode. But
the most likely Texas publisher said no—there was no point in
publishing letters of a writer who wasn't well-known. (True also
of a memoir, I'm sure. Why are you reading this?)

The Baylor job was good enough that for almost four full academic years I stayed fairly content. I had good students, and Nell and I found a church we both liked: Lakeshore Baptist, which to my mind was unBaptistlike in every important way, and especially in its young pastor, whose name I think was Richard Groves. He was quiet, dignified, and not only intelligent but intelligent enough not to talk down to a congregation that was heavy on professors from Baylor, which is of course a Baptist school. We had a nice house with neighbors we liked. It was a generally pleasant four years—minus a couple of months. In the spring of that last year came the news that *Playboy* magazine planned to do a story on Baylor girls. The president of the university, Abner McCall, let it be known that any Baylor girl who posed for *Playboy* would be disciplined. That edict did not please the student editors of *The Lariat*. They expressed what the statement at the top of the editorial page said the opinions on that page represented: those of the editors and not of the administration. Use your own judgment about posing, they advised students in an editorial. Thus crossed, Dr. McCall fired the student editors and removed their scholarships. I resigned in protest, effective at the end of the semester, but the journalism department, led by Gould, told me no, scram right now. I'm sure they didn't want my subversive presence influencing the remaining students. It was early April 1980. Nell and I collected my pay for the rest of the semester and scrammed to Bavaria and England—a very nice vacation. One other member of the journalism department, Dennis Hale, also resigned. Gould and the rest kept their jobs. I resented them not standing by the students and quitting in a body, but these days I come nearer to understanding that they had their livings to consider, their families to feed. I wasn't worried on that score, as I had never been. I could find a job.

I did so without trouble. The *Playboy* episode, including my resignation, drew publicity, of course, and I soon had an offer to teach journalism at the University of Mississippi. We went happily to Oxford, a place Nell and I enjoyed for different reasons. I felt the Faulkner presence looming over every block of the town, and I had students with more creativity than any I had had elsewhere, not to say that all of them were finished writers. Nor were they fully literate—what did you expect? The one exception to that, and one of the two students of my teaching career who showed perfect English usage, was a young woman named Kitty Dumas. She was cute, shy, and, at that university where students had so fervently protested the admission of James Meredith, black. I was happy to learn, years later, that she was running a successful public relations firm in Florida.

Also, in that one year at Ole Miss, I made a lasting friend in another journalism professor, a classic Southern gentleman named Jere Hoar, and got acquainted with a visiting celebrity, Willie Morris. I think Nell had a still better year than I. She went to work as a reporter for *The Oxford Eagle*. Some of her assignments were to interview Morris and the writer-friends that he brought to the campus. Among them were William Styron and James Dickey. Interviewing Dickey, Nell remarked that she had admired the passage from his novel *Deliverance* in which the protagonist climbs a cliff. Dickey leaned back in his chair, slapped his thigh and said, "Wasn't that good?"

Near the end of our year in Oxford, Nell got word from her mother that the weekly paper in Miami, Texas, was for sale. That is the very small Panhandle town in which both of Nell's sets of grandparents lived when she was a child. She loved the place, and I remembered it as hilly and picturesque. We couldn't resist. For seven months, we—mostly Nell, while I worked on my first book—put out *The Miami Chief* with equipment of about Model T Ford vintage. Later, with much of the observation coming from Nell, I wrote about a couple of Miami people. One was Thurman Chisum.

—Thurman lived just down the Main Street hill
from us, so we saw him all the time, propped up
and snipping in his yard or even down on hands
and knees, almost prone, wearing black leather
pads on his knees and digging weeds. He had the
nice roses, several apricot trees whose blossoms
usually got browned by a mid-April frost, and the
thick hedge of purple lilacs, which for a few days
in spring we couldn't walk past without stopping
and backing up a step to relocate their wonderful
smell. He had tomato plants, and in August, when
we had just moved to town and were spending long
hours at the paper, we would come home late at
night and find that he had left a half-gallon plastic
pail of cherry tomatoes on our doorstep. To do
that, he had had to shift his weight to his feet, pick
up the walking frame, set it down a few inches up
the slope, lean over it, and bring one foot and then
the other forward till they were together, and he
could start again. Moving like a round-shouldered
mechanical man with rusted joints, he had gone
through the procedure enough times to get him
the steep half-block up to our door, carrying the
tomatoes the Lord knows how.

   He had lived in Miami all his life. People there,
he told us, had always been mighty nice to him.
He said one woman, whose yard he used to care
for, would come to her door after he had worked
all morning and say, "Thurman, your lunch is
ready." Telling about it, he imitated the voice with
its tone of motherly commendation and of joy in
giving good tidings. He told the rest of the story:
he worked all afternoon, and then she came to

the door again. "Thurman," she said in the same beatific tone, "your supper is ready." The story was over, and he smiled, waiting for us to show our pleasure, too.

Another of our readers was Jewel Rogers, a widow in her seventies who wore a gimme cap, gray sweatpants, and running shoes and who operated her own small ranch.

—She walked into *The Chief* one day carrying a Spiral notebook. She stood at the counter, which came up to her chin—or, rather, which her chin bent down to; she would be small even if her spine were straight, and arthritis had made her smaller yet. She handed Nell the notebook. She had written a letter to the Amarillo paper, she said, and she wanted Nell to put "some foxy words" in it.

Her letter scolded farmers for (it said) hollering poverty all the time they were working in air-conditioned tractors and taking expensive trips to demonstrations in Washington. It said she remembered a different kind of farm life: *I have spent my life watching for a rain. When a cloud came up, we would all line up in the yard to see what it was going to do. When we saw it was headed east, my dad would say, "We won't go hongery. We have a plenty to live on. We just don't have any money."*

Nell told her the words looked plenty foxy to her. She typed the letter, fixing the spelling and punctuation, and gave it back.

Two Sundays later, the letter appeared in the Amarillo paper, with a cartoon of a woman hollering, not very logically, "Wolf! Wolf!" We clipped the letter to save for the writer and went to church. Just as the organist was finishing the introit, Jewel came in, out of breath. She headed straight for us, squirmed past the others in the pew, sat down next to Nell, hugged her, and said this was the most exciting thing that had ever happened to her—the letter coming out with her name on it, and the cartoon, and all. When the preacher started talking, she restrained herself, but her mind was not on the service. She fumbled through the hymnal for the opening hymn, found it, and lost it. She tried for it again with unsteady hands, distracted. As she fumbled, Nell distinctly heard her breathe a four-letter word. (These two passages are from a story of mine that was published in *The Canyon News*.)

Nell had a wonderful time in Miami, but the town was just too small to support a paper that would support its owners. It wasn't too small for news, though. Just outside of town, in a grassy strip along the road, a young hitchhiker stabbed his male companion to death one night. When he had been convicted of a much lesser charge than murder, I rode with him in the sheriff's car, on the way to prison. The column I wrote for the *Chief* about that experience won me one of the few prizes of my writing life: second place in the annual Ernie Pyle Awards, sponsored by the Scripps-Howard newspapers. Part of my glory was the rubbed-off kind: the first-place winner was the well-known columnist, Mike Royko. There was no money, though, just the prize. And the trip to Cincinnati to accept that and to speak to the audience of mostly editors was all at my expense. "I have melancholy news," I told them. "*The Miami Chief* is no more." Nell and I had seen starvation lurking and had given up the paper, though unable to find any buyer with a death wish and maybe a few hundred dollars.

We went to Amarillo and rented a small, cheap house. I

kept on writing my book. Nell worked as, supposedly, a secretary to John Alpar, a noted ophthalmological surgeon whose erudite literary and musical allusions, torrential energy, and unyieldingly Hungarian pronunciation of Greek medical terms made her job really that of quasi-translator, advisor, and calmer-down. She loved the job, and her boss became a loyal friend of hers and mine. He died of COVID in the fall of 2021, in his mid-nineties, several months after undergoing respirator treatment and being sent home. His wife, Elizabeth, who died some years before him, had charm of a distinctly European-lady kind, gracious, warm, attentive, and understanding.

They, with a baby, had fled Hungary in 1956, during the nation's revolt against communism. When they had stepped across the border, safe at last, Elizabeth realized that she had dropped her diaper bag. John went back across the border, retrieved it, and escaped again. Once, his mother came to Amarillo to visit. Hungary by then had been occupied successively by Germans, Russians, and Americans. We asked her, hopefully, what it had been like under the Americans. "An occupying army is an occupying army," she said. (That reminded me of what the British said about American troops during the war: "overpaid, overfed, oversexed, and over here.")

John came to my Lieder recitals and always said they were "vonderful," though I know now that I had sung badly. He also taught me something about Hungarian. When I said that Nell and I had been to a Leontyne Price recital, he said "I have never heard him." Oh, I said, I mean the soprano. Elizabeth laughed and explained to me that Hungarian pronouns don't distinguish between the sexes. John never stopped saying "he" for "she." The Hungarian word for either, he says, is ő.

I forget how I found out that the owners of *The Pine Bluff Commercial* were looking for a managing editor. By then, I had finished my book manuscript and needed a job. Off to Arkansas, where the barbecue was pork instead of beef and people said of something they hadn't done right, "I called myself doing that." The editor and part owner, Edmond W. Freeman, III, was a burly, white-whiskered man who wore a suit and tie, spoke with plantation-owner formality, and applied ethical standards to his newspaper that Benjamin Franklin would have endorsed. We covered friends, enemies, and ourselves with the same fullness and the same uncommitted tone. We ran letters to the editor exactly as received, typos, solecisms, and all.

Subject to such standards, I had full charge of the newsroom. Though Edmond kept the title of editor for himself, he didn't look at stories or headlines before they were published, and he questioned me only once about a policy I had established: including in obituaries at least the general cause of death, as in "after a long illness." Why did I want that? he asked. Just because it's something I always wonder about when I read an obituary, I said, expecting him to demur. "Oh," he said, "all right, then." He was the only altogether ethical owner-editor I encountered in my whole career. His high standards, though, didn't apply to newsroom equipment. The typewriters balked; the furniture creaked. One day, Gwen Crownover, the small and feisty assistant city editor, picked up her chair, which had just flipped her over, and slammed it into the top of a wastebasket. I think Edmond and his brother, Armistead, the co-owner, must have been sparing expense because they planned to sell the paper soon.

Economy applied also to newsroom salaries, and yet we had a staff of fourteen willing and generally able reporters and editors. As at Ole Miss, real talent sometimes appeared in their work. Jane Gore told about an old woman's recollections of old-time music. When the subject came up, Jane reported, the woman tilted her chair back, looked at the ceiling in rapt memory, and raised her clasped hands. "It was great heaps better than what you hear these days,' she said." Recognizing a distinctive quote and using it right, with the setting also brought to life, are among the most valuable abilities in a reporter.

As had been the case at Baylor, I might have stayed a long time at *The Commercial* if things had gone uneventfully. But one day, Edmond called the staff in and announced that the paper had been sold—to Donrey Media Group, which had the reputation of a mere moneymaking chain, unconcerned with quality. I knew I couldn't last long as a Donrey editor, and very shortly the crisis came. Our advertising manager, Charles H. Barnes, was fired. I assigned a reporter to do a full story on the situation, just as we would have done if Barnes had been a widely known executive of some other business, such as a bank. That was the *Commercial*'s way, and a prideworthy way it was. But the new Donrey publisher, Dan Smith, told the assigned reporter that we would use a full story about the new ad man and in it say nothing about the departure of his predecessor except that the new man "succeeds Charles H. Barnes as manager." I told Smith I couldn't order a reporter to write a story like that. "Then you can clean out your desk," Smith said. Goodbye, Pine Bluff.

Before I had gone in to argue with Smith about the assignment, I was sure what was going to happen. When it had happened, I sat back and quietly lectured Smith on newspaper ethics, making, I'm sure, no impression at all. The editor of a newspaper owned by a cheapskate, greedy chain—and such chains have now grown dominant in the field—is no editor but only a hireling in charge of keeping newsroom expenses down. To hell with standards.

I don't remember whether I applied for a job with *Newsday* or whether someone there read about my Donrey adventure and got in touch with me. I was hired as a "special writer," meaning approximately a Pfc. with feature writing as my Nonmilitary Occupational Specialty. Because, I'm sure, of my small-town background, I was assigned to the Riverhead bureau and not to the main office in Melville. That assignment meant that Nell and I could live in what passes for the countryside on Long Island. We found a house in Cutchogue, amid vineyards and vegetable farms. The children were on their own—Andy in law school at the University of Texas, Betsy working as a secretary for a law firm in Dallas.

We felt almost at home on the East End. We were among people who were close to the soil, and we attended a small, white-frame Presbyterian church that I think dated to the 1700s and that had a gentle, up-in-years pastor, George Borthwick, whom we quickly came to love. At work, I often wrote the Long Island Diary, which was essentially a personal column without "I." One subject was the piano of the late composer Douglas Moore, who had lived a few hundred yards from our place. He composed in a cabin at the edge of a creek near his house. After his death, vandals had dragged his old upright piano outside, possibly meaning to haul it off but having to abandon it for some reason. When I went to look, the piano's corpse was standing atilt on the uneven ground. I wrote about it in a Diary:

—No squirrel is going to wake the woodland by
running up and down the keyboard. The keys are
a pile of kindling, and besides, the bent and broken
hammers, exposed because the whole wooden
abdominal wall of the piano is gone, are poised at
such cockeyed angles they couldn't strike even if the
accumulation of twigs and leaves among the rusty
strings would let them. . . . The other day, a bough
tipped with a cluster of red oak leaves, survivors
from last fall, hung over the piano, making a
picture of nature dominating art. A flock of
honking geese flew past on the way from the North
Fork Country Club to the creek. Surely Moore's
operas have goose calls in them.

Another Diary of mine was about the return of Junior, a harbor seal, to the sea after nearly nine weeks of living in a tank at Okeanos, an ocean research foundation on the south shore, and being treated for the lungworms that had nearly killed him. I rode with him back to the sea. At Shinnecock Inlet he was set down on the sand in his straitjacket-like wire cage. When he heard the surf, he was so excited that he squirmed himself around in the cage like a jelly-filled balloon to face toward home. They set him on the sand in his cage. He stuck his head out, looked left and right, squirmed the rest of the way clear of the cage, and flumped toward the surf. He was so fat that with each flump the back part of his body rolled forward and settled onto the sand after the front part. Back in the water at last, he swam unseen for a while and then surfaced at the top of a wave as if to have one last look at the people who had made him well.

I'm pretty sure I wrote the Diary more often than anyone else during my stay, and still I once got a note asking if I could please turn in more copy. There and elsewhere, I worked as hard as anybody when the work presented itself, but I was never particularly good at turning up ideas on my own. Why not? Laziness, I think. Maybe it reflected my too-easy years in grammar school. Maybe it only reflected itself. At any rate, the two years with *Newsday* were good ones, partly because of the expertness all around me. The most memorable example of that was the writing coach, Harvey Aronson, who edited my copy and made or suggested changes only twice—of a single word, which I wish I could remember, and of a weak lead. To my mind, forbearance is a desirable quality in an editor, and a rare one. Like most writers, I've been harmed much more often than helped by editors.

When I go to New York these days, as I didn't do during COVID, I marvel that anyone, even a cab driver, can drive on those frantic streets. It must be my age. I used to drive with Nell from Cutchogue all the way to a parking garage near Lincoln

Center or Carnegie Hall or some pre-concert restaurant, cursing of course, but not quaking. Even though that was nearly thirty years ago, New York already had, you know, a fairly large population, some of which was fool enough, like me, to get onto the streets in its own car. We survived; we had a marvelous time. We went to operas, concerts, museums. At the Met, we heard and saw surely one of the best casts ever in *Le Nozze di Figaro*, which was Nell's favorite of the three great Mozart operas: Kiri Te Kanawa as the Countess, Kathleen Battle as Susanna, Frederica von Stade as Cherubino, Thomas Hampson as the Count, and I think José van Dam as Figaro. And I think James Levine conducting. Wow.

At Carnegie Hall, we heard a recital by Dietrich Fischer-Dieskau, the great German baritone, and though the music was all Hugo Wolf, without a note of Schubert, Schumann, or Brahms, I sat forward in my seat the whole time—and not just because I had been placed behind a pole. Good days, the Long Island ones. I even went fishing a couple of times, once catching my biggest fish, a six-and-a-half-pounder of the species that Texans call sea trout but that New Yorkers call weakfish. It had remarkably little meat on its bones, and that was of remarkably little flavor. Other things on Long Island had flavor indeed—the fresh strawberries, the vegetables (though no black-eyed peas) off the little farms, and especially the wonderful ears of delicate white corn, sweeter even than what my granddad used to grow.

Texas called again. We got close; we moved to Kansas, where I had a job as the writing coach and a once-a-week columnist for *The Wichita Eagle*. That was my last job, and the best, and it lasted the longest—almost nine years. The staff was so talented that the coaching part of my job was a pleasure. I did a written critique of the paper every morning and went through reporters' stories with them whenever they asked. Nobody was *sent* to me for coaching. The editor, W. Davis (Buzz) Merritt, ruled that out. Otherwise, he told me, other reporters might say, "Aha, he must not be doing good work." Buzz was a wise, judicious, quietly impassioned editor. The dominance of newspapers among "the media" was slowly dying during my time at the *Eagle*, as I in my happy years there barely realized but that Buzz saw with a sadness that has grown since his retirement. Besides coaching, my job was the weekly column, often about outdoor Kansas, including my favorite part, the lovely green Flint Hills. Nell and I took a memorable drive into them, starting at Cassoday:

—The hills emerge only as you drive north from
there, and then rather suddenly. They always make
me wonder why I didn't see them from several miles
away. I think the answer is that they aren't so much
true hills, heaped up above the general level of the
land, as bas-relief ones—hills mainly by virtue of
their valleys. You drive down into the hills.

I also did an occasional feature or news story, including a badly overwritten one on Bob Dole, the Kansan who was the Republican presidential nominee in 1996. Nell had a part-time job at an ophthalmological clinic that was an easy walk from our house, even for her, when her lifelong problem with flat feet and arthritis had become bad enough that for the first time she started using a cane. She loved her job; she loved all the jobs she ever had and was loved and respected on all of them. At the paper, my most frequent coachee was a young business reporter, Guy Boulton. He and I have remained close friends. His modesty, kindness, and generosity were such that Nell once told me she had known just two saints in her life, and he was one. (The other was a Baptist missionary, Lillie Mae Hundley, whose small "As-told-to" memoir, called *While It Is Yet Day*, Nell virtually wrote for her.) I had long since done a canonization of my own, but of course she would never have included herself.

Wichita had books and arts. There was Watermark Books, a fine independent store that is still in business; and Wichita State University had on its faculty one of the nation's best poets, Albert Goldbarth, several of whose books I reviewed for the *Eagle* as they came out. Nell and I went to music almost as often as we had in New York. The Wichita Symphony was good, there were good soloists at WSU, and both Kansas City—the Missouri one—and the University of Kansas brought in recitalists, one of whom was Matthias Goerne, who was then in his comparative youth and had the most beautiful baritone voice I have ever heard. We also heard, twice, the great mezzo Frederica von Stade, who shared one of her recitals with the casually polished baritone Thomas Hampson—both of them known to us already from the wonderful *Nozze di Figaro* at the Met. I did think von Stade had a silly presence as a recitalist, giggling to the audience about what a handsome singing companion she had. Possibly she said "Hampson" instead of "handsome," but that didn't excuse the giggliness. Man, though, couldn't she sing. He, too.

In one of my columns, I complained about the meaninglessness of the invariable, unanimous standing ovations at the Wichita Symphony. What can you do when the music has been glorious, the greatest ever, I asked—stand on each other's shoulders? At the next symphony concert, about a third of the audience stayed seated to applaud—one of the few times I've observed a clear response to something I've written. But after another concert or two, everyone was standing up again. Sic transit.

I had finished my first book, a bit of World War II history that took place in the Texas Panhandle, and during the years with *The Eagle* I found time to do much research on a new book. The research consisted mainly of hiking above timberline in all the U.S. mountain ranges that had timberlines. I was in my sixties; I had a great time. I made a lasting literary friend, too: Alexander Drummond, a back-country, high-mountain skier who lived alone in a cabin above Ward, Colorado. He had been publications director for the National Center for Atmospheric Research in Boulder; was working on a book when I met him. For years thereafter, he and I wrote or e-mailed each other frequently and at length. He wrote fiction, nonfiction, and poetry, much of it brilliant, and tried scarcely at all to get it published, though I begged him to do so. I've known other writers, a few, who write only for their own satisfaction. Their example shames me, but it doesn't stop me from pushing my stuff as hard as I know how. The Depression, again?

Now and then, also, and not in connection with the book, I drove to Colorado or flew to Utah for skiing, sometimes with one or both of my children. On the first of those trips, to Utah, I was smitten for some reason with scruples of a kind that arises, maybe, from memories of the Depression and, maybe, from being sixty-four years old. I confessed in my column for *The Eagle*:

—Are we really supposed to ski? What good is skiing? It's not as if we were Snowshoe Thompsons delivering the mail over the crest of the Sierra on ten-foot homemade skis. No question about the value of that, supposing we're supposed to get mail. But how can we justify mindless and unproductive activity?... I'll tell you, it's almost enough of a distraction to interfere with the pleasure when the Protestant ethic skis along behind you and keeps calling out softly, "Neat turn, but you're wasting time, you know."

I survived my conscience and had a wonderful time. A few years later, when Nell and I were still living in Wichita, I cast conscience aside again and went to Colorado to hike and fish. As I was walking back to the car toward the end of a day, I saw movement in undergrowth ahead of me. I stopped and looked. It looked at me, too—a full-grown black bear. We went our ways, still eyeing each other. That gave me a bit for my column, of course: "I wonder if the bear went home and said, 'Guess what I saw?'" And once, when I had interviewed two skiers and a snowboarder on a slope above Berthoud Pass and was walking and running back down to my car, "I got slammed in the flank," I wrote in my column, "by the field marshal of all that day's gusts."

—And there went my hat, the good old cloth hat
that had shaded my eyes on my way to work for
many a dutiful season. It scudded straight across the
slope. I chased it a few steps and gave up—when I
ran that hard, I sank into the snow up to my knees.
But my hat skimmed along, as light as a freed spirit.

After a few seconds it flipped onto its brim and
without the slightest change of direction spun for
the shoulder of the mountain. It whirled faster and
faster, the way a skier gains speed when he schusses
a steep slope. Directly in its course, a rock stuck a
few inches out of the snow. Behind the rock, the
slope kinked sharply down, too steep for me to see.

When the hat hit the rock, it bounded into
the air like a jackrabbit taking a last look at the
pursuers it has left behind. Then it dropped over
the edge, out of sight forever. I turned and ran the
rest of the way to the car, laughing harder than
before. Though I hated to lose the hat, somehow I
was delighted that it had escaped so spectacularly.
It was as if a small, wild part of me had decided
the devil with convention, it wasn't leaving the
mountains ever again.

I loved writing my column for those years, and Nell and I felt at home in Wichita except when we heard the kind of pronunciation that makes all the rhyming vowels in "Rock Chalk, Jayhawk" exactly the same as the one in "Rock." Wichita, being much lower in altitude, was hotter in summer than Amarillo, and being farther north and farther inland, colder in winter. Still, it was a plains climate and a plains populace. We might have stayed longer except for two things: (1) a new editor came in, one who didn't see a need for a writing coach and planned to put me on the night copy desk, and (2) we were well into retirement age. Texas, here we come again.

Canyon has about thirteen thousand residents, though I'm not clear as to how the student population of West Texas A&M University is counted. The town is sixteen miles south of Amarillo. And it is twelve miles west of Palo Duro Canyon, from which, long before the state park existed, Canyon took its name. It is entertaining to drive a newcomer to the canyon. For nearly all of those miles, the countryside is farm, ranch, and wind turbine land, flat and without distinctive features except for the one turbine, which belongs to the university and is said to be the tallest in the United States. A little inside the gate to the park, though, a scene bursts open like the great breathless chords before the "O Freunde" solo in Beethoven's Ninth. It is truly a magnificent view, and the more so for its unexpectedness. I first saw it in our Memphis days, when I was eight or nine. We drove down what was then the new road, built by CCC personnel before my dad's days in the organization. At the bottom, Bob and I stood at the side of the jump-across creek that for eons had delicately nibbled sand, grass, and rock to cut that splendid gash into the plains. We took in the scene, certainly, but I, at least, was mainly interested in the ochre rocks alongside the creek, some of which I took back to Memphis to streak my face with—like, I imagined, an Indian brave.

Braves must in fact have made use of the ochre. The canyon was home, shelter, and hunting ground to groups of Comanches

and Kiowas until September 28, 1874, when soldiers under Colo-
nel Ranald Slidell Mackenzie ran them out and made them go to
the reservation at Fort Sill, Oklahoma. Soon the canyon became
part of the 1.3 million-acre JA Ranch. The ranch owner, Charles
Goodnight, had as stony a front as the red-rock east wall of the
canyon but was also a visionary, and he was married to another,
Molly Goodnight. They kept enough of the native bison alive to
provide the herd of great beasts that now cause visitors to Cap-
rock Canyons State Park, sixty miles or so to the south, to stop
their cars and wait until the herd decides to meander ponderous-
ly off the narrow road. There are no buffalo in Palo Duro Can-
yon anymore, only the three Longhorn cattle that graze behind
a fence just inside the park entrance and seem as placid as if they
were not armed with a large, menacing, and surely inconvenient
length of primeval horn.

What else the Palo Duro has is graceful little white-tailed
deer that do *grands jetés* across the road in front of your car, wav-
ing their luxuriant tails as blithely as if they had been just hoping
for a chance to do that. It also has flocks of wild turkeys, a large
populace of roadrunners whose surprisingly dovelike mating
calls echo through the canyon on an early morning in spring,
a number of wary and camouflaged aoudad sheep on the steep
canyon walls, and coyotes that yammer and keen at sundown
in packs that sound like thirty and are probably five or six. The
Palo Duro is in the class of Pikes Peak as a natural attraction to
have close by. Part of being ninety is that I don't try hiking the
steeper trails there anymore, but I still enjoy doing a couple of
miles on a leveler one that zigzags along the course of the little
trickly creek that created the whole scene and that is officially
the Prairie Dog Town Fork of the Red River.

The main thing about Canyon, though, was that it was
home. It was the Panhandle, it was close to Amarillo, where Nell
and I had met and lived, and it was an easy drive from Pampa,

where her mother still lived. We were old, by some standards, but I, at least, approaching seventy when we arrived, could walk more than four miles in an hour and could still enjoy skiing at Taos, a half-day's drive to the west. Lord knows how much pain Nell's formless feet and sagging ankles were giving her by then, but she loved being home again. When we were leaving Wichita, she had said to me, "I can't think of anyone I'd rather grow old with." I told her neither could I. We had picked out a lot at the southeast city limits of Canyon, with a three-mile view of pasture and crop land out what would be our back window, and we told the house builders to put in a chain link fence back there, not a tall board one, so we could enjoy that view.

The house, built according to Nell's sensible and thrifty stipulations, was smaller than others in the neighborhood, but it had plenty of room for us and two extra bedrooms for visitors. It also had, by my instructions, an old-fashioned storm cellar in the backyard. I used it as a wine cellar for a couple of years, but we also put it to its intended use twice, once when the TV showed a tornado coming from the west and practically inside the Canyon city limits. Our next-door neighbors joined us underground that time, but when we dared to stick our heads out, we found that our houses were still there—the storm had changed course. The other time, it was just the two of us, and a briefer, lesser threat. In those days, Nell could still back down the steep wooden stairs into the cellar. Fortunately, she never needed to try later, when she certainly couldn't have made it; I would have had to go halfway down and try to drag her with me without breaking her bones or mine. We should have foreseen that difficulty and put in a more easily entered cellar.

In the same way, we never thought, at house-building time, that the bathroom doorways would need to be wide enough for a wheelchair. The time came when we had to have one of those doors widened, and even so, there was only a quarter inch to spare on each side; I had to aim carefully when I pushed the wheelchair through. But that problem arose only toward the end of Nell's years in the house. For ten or twelve years, she used first a cane and then a walker. She got around well enough that way to enjoy travel with me.

We took a second trip to Germany and England. In a small shop in Germany, Nell, using her cane, fell on the concrete threshold, breaking a tooth and bruising her face so badly it was black the rest of our trip. She got immediate and skillful medical and dental treatment in Germany, though not so, later, in England, where the nurse who removed her stitches had failed to wash her hands and so caused a small infection. Nell never complained. She admitted only once that she was in pain on that trip, and that when I had asked her outright. We bought her a walker right away in Germany, a *Gehbock*. That was the end of her cane-using days.

In the Panhandle, the sky is scenery. Many a time, we stood at the back window of an evening and saw sunlight seeming to radiate from the golden-tan grass in the pasture while the blackest storm cloud loomed over the whole sky behind it. Then, as likely as not, a rainbow would appear. Again, at sundown, the wispy clouds would take on the subtlest suggestion of wild-plum purple—the atmospheric event that Nell enjoyed the most, I think. She loved mere hints of color, loved little things. For one of our anniversaries or of her birthdays, I forget which, I gave her a little gold "horned toad" (a lizard, really, but never mind). I had had a small red ruby put in its forehead, and of course she immediately caught the allusion: "Sweet are the uses of adversity, / Which, like the toad, ugly and venomous, / Wears yet a precious jewel in his head."

That wasn't the only literary connection the little reptile had. In Mark Twain's retranslation of the French version of his "Celebrated Jumping Frog of Calaveras County"—or at least in our joint and somewhat inaccurate memory of it—one character says to another, "My God, Smiley, I no see not that that frog has anything of better than every frog." So "every frog" became Avery Frog, which we shortened to Avery. "Want to wear Avery tonight?" I would ask when we were going out to dinner, and she usually did.

Nell's wit, until her last year or two, was terse and amazingly quick. Once, when we saw a perfectly circular house, I asked her, "People who live in round houses should not throw...?"

"Square dances," she said instantly.

In the house, thumb-tacking a large world map onto the wall, I remarked that it was a shame to waste the wide, empty margins. What could we put there? Without a second's thought:

"Here Be Dragons."

She loved the round, orange moons when they were just coming into sight through the latticed elm limbs at the edge of the pasture and had not yet shrunken in their climb. Until she became too weak to stand up, she would come over from her chair and look with me. The sky was the setting of our love—it, and the plains.

The word plains, to my mind at least, does not apply to farmland. Cotton plants, when "hung with snow" of the kind that irrigation produces, are a pleasant sight for their own sake and also for the comfort and security you know they are promising for some farm family. The same is true of corn, though the elephants to which the stalks are eye-high must have for economical reasons become smaller and smaller. Wheat, in its stages from low green in the fall to tall green in the spring and then to the light brown that bespeaks loaves of crusty bread, makes a landscape nearest to plains, but, especially when irrigation devices show human intent, can't quite sustain the role. Crops, yes, can be pleasant to see. Still, they aren't the plains. Plains are essentially grass, whether green or, more often, brown, and whether dense or, much more often, sparse and clotted by yucca and mesquite. Plains support cattle, though very few per thousand acres, and to see a herd with heads down, grazing, arouses an Old Testament contentment in me. Surely it would do the same if I were an unbeliever or a vegetarian. Nell, too, though most of her family land was cultivated, felt a close and satisfying connection to the plains.

On my daily walks within the Canyon city limits, I make a circuit of a vacant lot from which I can see across several miles of pasture, usually with a few cattle in view. The openest and most distant part of the view is an uninhabited expanse that seems to lift gently into the air, into unimpeded distance. At my first sight of it, daily, I breathe deeply and involuntarily, and I realize how shallowly and tensely I had been breathing until then. Lungs must have eyes, or is it that brains have lungs?

When the plains roughen up, as, for instance, on the route northwest from Amarillo to Boys Ranch, they may strictly speaking not be plains anymore, but they affect me the same way, and then some. So it's not just the potentiality of juicy steaks that gives grassland its charm—rough country isn't as productive for grazing as flat country. It must be the sense of wildness, the mystery, the possibility of challenge and danger behind the next rise or in the next canyon. We like to scare the instinctive side of ourselves as long as our reasoning side knows we're perfectly safe. So we ride roller coasters or sky dive, or we drive through the breaks in the Texas Panhandle.

The plains aren't for everybody. My son and daughter, who live, respectively, in Houston and Massachusetts, do not love Panhandle land. They want trees, want greenery and water. I understand; I like those things, too. Elizabeth, since she has multiple sclerosis, suffers more than the ordinary from hot weather. Summers in Texas, even my part of Texas, would set her back. We all keep hoping that this or that latest experiment in

MS treatment will prove effective and become available to her. Meanwhile, she gets around well if not rushed, and she writes her legal analyses full-time and profitably from her house on a pretty little lake—called a pond or maybe a "great pond" in that verdant place west of Boston. Andy, with his lawyer-wife and two delightful grown daughters, loves living in Houston in spite of the summers. At the mention of places with real winters, I believe he gets a mental image of South Dakota and the car in the snowdrift, with an icicle-dripping diagonal line slashed through the image. Both of my children have prospered as lawyers, and much beyond that, have shown such mature wisdom and world knowledge that it is I who usually seek advice from them rather than the other way around. It was not that way with me and my parents, and just as well.

It may be—probably is—that my response to bare brownness is considerably shaded by the fact that it was in that setting that I met Nell and came to love her. And came to lose her. The view from my walking route has sadness to it now, along with the lung-filling serenity of old. Nell may have been the one lifetime woman companion decreed for me, and possibly also the only one whom I not only would love and almost worship through the many years but also would be accepted by, would be the right one for her to grow old with. We were walking back to our hotel from an opera in Chicago and a nicely dressed man, probably in his sixties, and leaning on a wall, saw us looking happy and old together. What's your secret? he asked. "She'll put up with almost anything," I said, and he said he would remember that. It was true. When I told that story to Nell's mother, Edith Osborne, she nodded maybe a little too vigorously, as if to say yes, Nell has had to do that. As a matter of fact, Edith was a very sweet woman, and she and I got along nicely together. And anyway, she was right.

My kind of being ninety, like everybody else's kind, shows

a powerful influence of loss. Everybody who makes ninety has lost parents, siblings, and friends, and very likely also husband or wife. My three best friends on the *Star-Telegram*—John Mort, Jack Douglas, and Frank Friauf—died in their middle years of, mainly, cigarettes. Dick Phelan died of a revolver. My mother died in the middle 1990s of, or at least with, Alzheimer's disease. My dad died a few months after her, at the age of ninety-five. A few weeks before that, he asked me, "Did Betsy die?" Yes, I said. "I thought so," he said. His memory, not many days after that, began dragging its own art gum eraser behind it as it moved along, so that he would tell a story, finish it, and instantly start it over, again and again, like birdsong. I hope the memory of what I had had to tell him was also erased. I wonder if, when I am dying, I will have to ask one of my children the same thing about Nell. I know the answer well enough now.

Among her many afflictions, Nell began to be seriously depressed about ten years ago. One of our friends had said about her, earlier, "I wonder if there is anything Nell hasn't read." But she gradually stopped reading except for the funnies and "Dear Abby." She slept more and more, especially during the dark winters. She underwent a several-month manic spell in which she had sudden enthusiasms that she as suddenly dropped. She wanted a small car of her own, and when I brought one home for her, she got in, drove it once, and then lost all interest in it. She had delusions about tapped phone lines, about elaborate con games directed at us; was sure there were drug dealers in the city park visible from our house and that they thought we were watching them on behalf of the police. Sometimes she screamed at me—something, as with all of the other symptoms, utterly unlike her real self. "You never let me finish one sentence." "You never listen to one thing I say." It was one of the worst periods of my life. When winter approached, her usual depression began returning, and with the help of medicine from her psychiatrist she returned to normalcy, albeit of a gray kind. Her wonderful mind declined to the extent that she couldn't add three and two. Even so, she still had flashes of wry humor, and, amazingly, she knew big words and could tell me what they meant: ophidian, eschatology. Then she started having bad pain in her right shoulder. It was a tumor, and in an inaccessible place. The pain medicines our doctor was allowed to give her were inadequate.

I put her in a nursing home in Amarillo, where she was under hospice care with no limit to the strength and amount of pain medicine she could have. That meant she slept even more than before, but at least she didn't hurt so much. I sat in her room, translating Rilke poems, while she slept. Nell knew she was dying—she had heard the word "hospice" from a nurse—but neither of us said so. The intensity of our "I love yous" made it plain that we both knew. And yet, when a woman friend of ours was getting ready to leave after a visit, Nell woke up and gave her an open, sweet, grateful smile, the kind our friends had known and loved for years. On the morning of November 15, 2018, a nurse phoned me and said they had given Nell a shower and then the morphine she had asked for, and then she had stopped breathing. Nell is buried in our double plot. The cemetery is just south of Canyon. It is on the plains.

Before those last years with Nell, I wrote some of the poems and prose I had always wanted to write and considered it my duty to write. One of the poems was *Wolfe*, which is published under the same cover as these reflections, being, after all, an important event of my old age. I wrote it in a spirit of self-education. In keeping with my lifelong laziness about hard studies, I had never fully learned the grammar and vocabulary of Old English (also known as Anglo-Saxon). So I lacked a real appreciation of *Beowulf,* except for the wonderful sound of the language, and that sound was the foundation of my doctoral work.

After years of feeling guilty about my lack of comprehension, I decided to try to show myself what it was that had presumably made *Beowulf* a success with audiences of its time. In that attempt, I would move the Grendel episodes into a closer setting and time: the Texas Panhandle of the 1890s. And since mere monster-slaying was too shallow a core for current audiences—or so I thought, not being a moviegoer—I would supply an underlying theme: the wilderness's resistance to development. The ranchland equivalents of Grendel and his mother would embody that resistance and to a degree would be shown sympathy even by their mortal enemies, the ranchers and cowboys. The original poem showed some suggestion of that sympathy in a word that was used to characterize Grendel's lair: *wynleas*—joyless.

I knew better than to try to write *Wolfe* in the same meter as *Beowulf*, which simply doesn't work in modern English. Instead, I used a typical cowboy meter with four-stress iambic lines, dee-DUM, dee-DUM, dee-DUM, dee-DUM. And I used rhyming couplets, the same as in "The Old Chisholm Trail" or "I ride an old Paint." I don't know how many weeks I spent on the writing, but I remember that it came readily and that I was absorbed in it. When the poem was done, I sent it around to this magazine and that, and before long, it was accepted by *Rattle*, which ran the whole poem and then, at my suggestion, published it separately as a chapbook. The whole experience with *Rattle* was possibly the biggest break of my writing life. It was certainly one of the most gratifying.

After the chapbook, when I had regained the copyright, the poem was published, along with some of my short poems, by an ambitious young Londoner who pushed it, with very little success, as the work of a sure-enough Texan. His company went out of business in a couple of years. I am glad to have the poem in print now from a Texas publisher.

Another writing project of my old age is this chronicle,

which tries in part to show what it is like, being ninety and a widower. That is a question that the COVID invasion made possibly simpler, possibly more complicated, than it would otherwise have been. Being ninety under these circumstances was much like being any other age in that the lid on life had been screwed down tight since mid-March of the bad year, 2020. All of us who had any sense were in solitary for the duration. I kept reading online and seeing on TV that the virus was far more dangerous to me than it was to young people. As far as I knew I had no "underlying conditions" to intensify the danger. (If such a condition were underlying very deeply, would I know I had it?) But ninety is in itself a condition, whether underlying or overlying.

I kept on backing away from unmasked people in the grocery store, kept on washing my hands as hard as Lady Macbeth, kept on scratching my itchy nose with my shirt sleeve instead of my fingers. I don't want to die, not yet, or only if God will promise me that when I do, I will be reunited with Nell forever, in full consciousness and with full memory of our lives on Earth. Of course, if I should hear God make that promise to me, before I acted on it I would have to consider the possibility that I was going mad. But if so—I would surely wonder—what will the rest of my life be like? "Like that, huh? OK, thanks. Where did I put that revolver?"

Since I don't really expect God to speak to me as he has never spoken to any other person in all the time the world has been peopled, and since I imagine that if madness were going to start seeping out of its perhaps underlying place in my gray matter it would have done so before now, then my part is to keep on being ninety-plus the best I can for whatever more time is given me. Being ninety in COVID time, the same as being thirty in that time, meant being alone. For me, aloneness was productive, if not of joy, at least of time and desire to write. I had thought my creative faculty had grown too feeble to stir up more than, rarely, a small poem. But I probably wrote more verse in three quarantined months than I had in a year before the invasion. Much of it was about Nell, or, rather, about my feelings since she died: whines and groans rather than tributes. Still, something. And I've written an introduction to my Rilke translations, and, as always, lots of letters asking editors or publishers please to look at the enclosed.

And I've written this, whatever it amounts to. To an extent, I've tried to reveal myself. Only to an extent. As I wrote in an *Eagle* column, "my inner self belongs to the none-of-your-business school. . . . The virtue of privacy, to my mind, outweighs every imaginable virtue of display." Writing what I am now winding up has made me stop and try to think about my age and why I have attained it and what else I hope to do with it. The attempt hasn't been very successful. All I know for certain is that I'm here and I'm past ninety, and I'm not sure whether anything else is a matter of what I do with my nineties or of what my nineties do with me. So far, they have treated me better than I deserve.

ABOUT THE AUTHOR

Donald Mace Williams is a former writing coach for *The Wichita Eagle* and reporter and editor for papers that include *Newsday*, the *Fort Worth Star-Telegram* and the *Amarillo Globe-News*. He has taught English and journalism at West Texas State and Baylor Universities. Williams holds a doctorate in English from the University of Texas. He lives in Canyon, Texas, and his poetry has been published widely in journals in the United States.

Looking for your next book?

Check out our other titles, including audio books, at
StoneyCreekPublishing.com.

For author book signings, speaking engagements,
or other events, please contact us at
info@stoneycreekpublishing.com.

Stoney Creek Publishing

A Member of the Texas Book Consortium

We publish the stories you've been waiting to read.

CPSIA information can be obtained
at www.ICGtesting.com
Printed in the USA
JSHW021700170123
36202JS00001B/2

9 798986 407821